ADULTING 101:

*How to get your sh*t straight*
so you can succeed

Adulting 101:
How to get your sh*t straight so you can succeed

by

E. B. Davis II

Two Cat Press

2018

Cover designed by E.B. Davis II
Graphics by Justin Vazach
www.vazachdesign.com

E.B. Davis II
Visit my website at www.ebdavis2.com

Printed in the United States of America

First Printing: March 2018
Somerset163 Ltd
dba Two Cat Press
Columbus, OH

ISBN- 978-1-7321485-0-5

"However vast the darkness, we must supply our own light."
~ Stanley Kubrick

Dedication

I'd like to dedicate this book to one of my cats, Ziva. She unfailingly sat on my desk during this entire process, sometimes sticking her ass in my face, sometimes stepping on the keyboard and accidentally deleting my brilliant thoughts, generously shedding her fur into my coffee, and occasionally rolling over to show me her cute, round belly to distract me from my productivity. Without her, this book would have been done a few days earlier. With her, well, everything is better with her.

CONTENTS

A Thing You Should Know 6
Introduction 7
PRE-STEP: What the fuck is success exactly? 11
Section 1: Victim Mentality 26
Step 1: Stop Blaming Your Fucking Parents. 28
Step 2: Stop Blaming Everyone Else and Look in the Mirror, Dickhead 37
Step 3: Being depressed: Find a way to stop that shit. 50
Step 4: Stop Taking Everything So Fucking Personally 58
Section 2: Fantasy Thinking 68
Step 5: Stop Wishing Away Your Life 70
Step 6: The Grass Ain't Any Fucking Greener Over There 76
Step 7: Kill the Trolls in Your Head 82
Step #8: Obsess Much? 91
Section 3: Procrastinating 97
Step 9: Stop Fucking Doing Nothing. 100
Step 10: Tick tock, mother fuckers. 107
Time to Wrap This 117
Shit Up 117

A THING YOU SHOULD KNOW

This is a concept that is not only interesting but applies later...

Schrödinger's cat: a cat, a flask of poison, and a radioactive source are placed in a sealed box. If an internal monitor (e.g. Geiger counter) detects radioactivity (i.e. a single atom decaying), the flask is shattered, releasing the poison, which kills the cat. The Copenhagen interpretation of quantum mechanics implies that after a while, the cat is simultaneously alive and dead. Yet, when one looks in the box, one sees the cat either alive or dead, not both alive and dead. This poses the question of when exactly quantum superposition ends and reality collapses into one possibility or the other.

INTRODUCTION

I just finished this. At 5:57am, I declared the manuscript, save the introduction, finished. I have nothing more to say right now on this subject. I hope that I have made myself clear. Holy shit, I just sounded like my mother.

Here is how I got to this point:
I was sitting at this damn desk, pissed off at all the bullshit going on and I don't mean the aforementioned Ziva on her perch. This book was spurned by a specific person on social media who shall remain nameless.

People, including my nameless muse, who are in really shitty situations, situations worse than mine and they don't seem to have any fucking idea how they got there really need to hear these words and listen to them because it's like they looked up and said, "Huh. This is new. How did this happen? My life fucking sucks and I don't know what happened. I don't know my own story," and that makes me want to beat them about the face and head.

You don't know the story? You WROTE the fucking story, asshat.

"How did this happen?" I ask, rhetorically to the digital lives in my computer, often with a guffaw of disbelief. It is easy to see the forest for the trees when it ain't your forest.

"How did you get in this fucking mess? You literally have no idea? Or you metaphorically have no idea? Because it seems pretty obvious to me. Get your head out of your fucking ass and fix the fucking problem(s)." Yet, you cannot fix the problems if you don't know what they are.

I say that and think, "It really is that simple" but simple can be deceptively hard when looked at as a whole. Simple is easy if you've done it before. You know how, when you are learning something new, the person teaching you says, "Look, it's easy..." and you are all, like, "Yeah, to YOU because you have been fucking doing this for years!" I know I feel this way sometimes: I get overwhelmed when I view the 'thing' as a whole. "It's too much!" and I immediately plop my ass on the couch and start binge-watching some shitty show I don't even care about over Amazon Prime or Netflix or Hulu. You know you do that, too. Don't lie.

Anecdote time!
During a challenging period of my life, **cough** from my teens to about 32 **cough** someone said to me, "If you want to be happy, just be happy" and I thought that was the worst fucking advice I had ever been given in my entire life, and trust me, I was pretty good at asking for advice and then never fucking taking it.

"Just be happy"?

That simple, huh? Just *stop* being unhappy and *start* being happy. As in, just making a decision to do so and then I will be happy?

Seems legit.

But, you see, I get hung up on the how. *How* do I just be happy? What is the *process*? Can that be broken down for me into a series of steps that I can easily take and just follow along, ticking off the boxes on a pre-made to-do list?

Short answer: no, fuckhead.

Long answer: this book.

We are all going to follow along with the ten things I've had to deal with to get my head straight, that I've been following myself with some measure of success to get some shit done. Since people really seem to like having check lists and things laid out for them in an easy-to-digest manner, that is what I am going to do for you bunch of freakazoids. I mean, really. Let's be serious. Do you really have any fucking intentions at all to do something with yourself or are you just going to be content to read about it and then fantasize about how great it could be if only something magical happens that you don't have to work for?

We all love a rags-to-riches story but that's what they are: stories. They are modern day fairy tales or some fucked up perseverance porn. These things do happen but they are one-in-a-million lightning strikes. You cannot base your life on a one-in-a-million lightning strike then think back after 70 years have gone by and wonder what the fuck happened.

You can do one of two things: you can read this book and my other book, How Not to be an Asshole, and think about what I am telling you, and hopefully follow the advice...you know, actually *do* the work. All of which is substantially less expensive and stigmatizing than seeing a therapist; or you can keep on doing what you've always done which is probably not much and keep on getting what you've always gotten, which is also probably not much. That's cool, too, but much like voting, you don't get to blame anyone but yourself for the outcomes, whether they be good or bad. That's all on you, my flaky friends.

I said that there were ten things. That's not entirely accurate. They are more like guidelines. (Does anyone else immediately think of Geoffrey Rush as Captain Barbosa when they hear that or is that just me?) Yeah, more like guidelines. Things to think about and consider. Things that you need to work through and critically examine how you process the information before you can begin to make the change toward something better. If you have no idea how to think critically, then I suggest you spend a little bit of time researching the matter. You cannot do this and not have that ability. I'm pretty sure that I will lose a vast majority of you just from this part alone and we haven't even made it to the beginning yet. Well, fuckity fuckballs.

Critical thinking can hurt a little bit at the start. It might make you cry because there is going to be a shit load of cognitive dissonance but it is the beginning of everything. The more you do it, the easier it gets, the faster it gets and the truer it gets and the happier things become. Mostly.

As we all already know, not many people really like to do the work. Well, get fucking used to it.

So, about ten guidelines, right? Guidelines, steps, items, 'things'. I don't know what to call them. They have a bunch of different names. These are concepts, constructs, goals, lessons, shit you gotta get straight, yo. After this page are all of the 'things' I have gone through to gain some clarity. What I won't tell you is that I am perfect at any of them. I still fuck up. I still catch myself falling back into old patterns and habits. The difference now is that I am fucking aware of my bullshit and can set about fixing it much faster. I have better boundaries and am able to determine when I am fucking up.

But before we get to the meat, let's have an appetizer of sorts. There is actually another step to this that should be first, like a pre-step. Let's start with that because it would be really fucking stupid of me to put a pre-step at the end of a book.

One more thing, to the person who inspired me through their really shitty life to start this second book, I would like to say thank you. Thank you for giving me the push to set aside other things in my life to write these words. They needed to be written and, in your own shitty way, you were my catalyst.

E.B. Davis II
February 16, 2018

PRE-STEP: WHAT THE FUCK IS SUCCESS EXACTLY?

Let's figure that out, shall we? Success as defined by fancy fucking dictionaries says that it is the achievement of a goal or an aim; could also be attainment of 'prosperity'; and then some sort of popularity like having a book that people like.

We have three things that those fancy-schmancy dictionaries just told us: met a goal, made some money, did a thing people liked or are a thing that people like.

Let's break it down now... (cue the music)

Met a Goal: What goals do you have?

Let's start small.

Did you get out of your fucking bed and make it to the bathroom so that you didn't piss yourself? Success! And, if you didn't make it to the bathroom because of health problems or physical limitations, no biggie, no shame.

Were you able to make a reasonable cup of coffee at home with simple ingredients and not spend nine fucking dollars on marketing and pretentious atmosphere? Success!

Don't get me wrong, I like a Thai Chi Latte...or wait, is it Chai Tea Latte? Whatever the fuck it is, it is tasty and a million grams of sugar and a complete waste of money but I like them anyway, I just don't like Starbucks. Unless I have a gift card. Then I like Starbucks. Better yet, go to a locally owned coffee shop and get their version.

Did you get to work on time? Success!

Did you not kill anyone? Success!

Did you make breakfast-for-dinner and not get shells in your eggs? Success!

Did you *start* writing the next great American novel? Success!

Having goals both large *and* small is key. If you haven't figured this out already on your own, it's probably because you are either too busy being busy, (we'll go over that in a minute) or you really don't give a rat's ass about any of this and would just rather complain.

Well, fuck that.

Fuck that to the end of the earth, I say.

Let Auntie EB help you with this. Have the person closest to you give you a Dumb Slap on the back of the head. Great.

Goals. We all like to score then we can say "Lookie what I did" and we glance around like four year-olds hoping that someone has noticed that we took a shit in the potty on our own or didn't get shells in our eggs. We want that recognition that comes from others, even if it is just a quick "Hey, rock on" and acknowledgment that you did something. I'm here to tell you that you need to fucking knock that shit off. Again, just don't. Okay? Just fucking don't. Again, chapter one of my first book How Not to be an Asshole, no one really fucking cares.

I can tell you this as a parent, that every time my son says, "Hey Ma, c'mere, lookit this...." I cringe but I go see what he has done and hopefully it is something creative like a drawing or a cool building with his Legos or whatever and not torturing the cat by totally encompassing the poor thing in a fortress made of pillows and blankets. Cats hate that shit. They do. It is just that they know which side their bread is buttered on, unless you have an asshole cat like we do and they come shooting out of the pillow and blanket fortress like a fucking mongoose on LSD, fucking teeth and claws and screaming. Nightmares for everyone! Have you ever seen a mongoose on LSD? Me neither but I can imagine it is much like our cat, 13.

The point of that mini-rant was that we really fucking like it when people are proud of us. The people we care about, that is. The problem is when you want those damn accolades from people who don't fucking matter. Why should you give a shit if that asshole fucker that you knew in 5th grade that bullied you but now is your 'friend' on social media likes your post? Maybe your mom didn't praise you enough and at the right times when you were little so that you have figured out how to be proud of yourself. (That's coming up, too.)

That's not success, that's not meeting a goal. That's being an attention hound and what useful, contributing-to-society's advancement have you created by doing that? You've done nothing. So, yea this is a book about how to get your head out of your ass and not suck at life, and so we need to start with the first bullet point of success: goals. Your goals for your daily life should not be how many likes you get on social media for some stupid post about not getting shells in your eggs. That's a given. No one cares. You should care, they are your eggs but that's as far as it should go. Eat fucking crunchy shelly eggs if you want, that's fine. To each their own, weirdo. All I'm saying is, don't add to the general malaise of our culture with shit no one cares about. It's all just fucking noise.

What goals should we care about? Well, what does anyone else care about that pertains to you? Not much but there are some biggies. Let's go over the Big Goals that anyone should have in their daily lives.

Are you being an asshole? Again, go back to HNTBAA and re-read that. Don't do those things listed in there. Are you going by that rule, you know, the one your auntie or your Me-maw told you? Here, I'll go over it again: If you don't have something nice to say, then keep your fucking pie-hole shut, you brain dead tool. This includes online.

Maybe Auntie or Me-maw didn't say it quite like that or maybe then did, and if so then you have some kick ass ladies in your family.

Unless you are a super close friend, the kind who can get in close and say to the friend without fear of them throwing you off the roof, then just don't fucking open your mouth and say words that hurt people.

If you are not being an asshole, success!

Are you doing what you should be doing to pay the bills, and contribute to your household or are you being a moochy asswipe, expecting others to pay your way? This is a big pet-peeve of mine. Contribute, fucksticks. If there is some sort of dystopian future and I am in charge of a compound or commune and everyone has to pitch in in some way and there's some lazy fuck who thinks that they can reap the rewards without fucking doing a damn thing... Oh, those people piss me off and I would surely throw their useless piece of shit living carcass to the zombies or the machines or the irradiated experiment-gone-horribly-awry giant pill bugs. (Pill bugs are also known as woodlouse, roly-poly, Butchy-boys (what the fuck?), doodle bugs, or in the case of my son up until about a year ago, Tiny Hipsters. I don't know why the hell he called them tiny hipsters. I just saw him out front, squatted down, poking at them. I said, "What are you doing?" He said, "I'm giving the tiny hipsters a home. They are homeless." Of course, I laughed my ass off because that was ironic, which was also ironic considering: hipsters; and just ... it was fucking funny, okay?)

Tiny hipster eating cat food.

Back to the point: are you contributing to your general area in a positive way? Yes? Success!

Let's keep these goals in perspective. I am in no way saying that you should not reach or aim for something more. Abso-fucking-lutely. Yes. Please. Aim high and all that bullshit. Be all you can be, yadda yadda yadda but I don't think that shooting for the moon is appropriate when you can't even get your fucking head right about what a proper goal is and whether or not it is successful. Let's keep it simple for now, morons.

For example, let us think that you'd like to write a book someday. Maybe a fiction novel about giant, irradiated, experiment-gone-wrong Butchy-boys who start slowly decomposing the world and before long, life as we know it is over. Sounds fucking fantastic. This is a goal. In order to be able to throw up your hands and say

"Success! I wrote a book about giant tiny hipsters" you first have to start smaller.

Are you writing daily? Do you write short stories? Are you studying plot formation? Do you know how to build a compelling character? Are you practicing?

◆ ◆ ◆

Anecdote Time!
Back to my kid, he loves to draw. He draws all the time, on everything. We were at the library and he was whining that he'd read or looked at all the books about cars that are available in our branch of the library. He wandered with me over to the section I was going to and saw some books about beginning character drawing. He has a ton of books he's drawn about his Stick Men, comics really, and some of them are fucking great, but he's ready to advance past stick drawings even though the ones he does have lots of detail in their movement. The kid gets it, ya know? Anyway, he gets the books, we go home and he starts to do the tutorials. He drew a mummy and it was a reasonable replica of the one in the book. Next, he tried a unicorn or some other magical creature and, well... not so much. He got super pissed and started to slam shit around. I said, "You've had that book for less than 15 minutes. You've tried once. Try again." And in my head, I'm thinking, "For FUCK'S SAKE! Give yourself a break, you're 8. Just try again and again and again and again until it gets better." He needs to practice the unicorn. The unicorn was harder than the mummy, it will require more practice. They call it Beginner's Luck for a reason. My auntie makes the best potato soup. I tried to make the same soup. It didn't turn out like hers. I was disappointed in myself but then I took my own advice and remembered that I probably made 300 batches (over time) of our family recipe for mashed potatoes before they started to taste like my mothers. I made one batch of soup. I have to keep practicing.

◆ ◆ ◆

In order to meet your big goals, you have to practice small goals on a daily basis. If you are not willing to put in the fucking work on a daily fucking basis to get the fucking basics down, then you are not going to achieve your fucking goals and you will be fucking upset with yourself, slamming your fucking shit around the kitchen and pissing everyone off.

Goals: Think small, act small, be content with little successes and don't look around to see if anyone noticed. Did you notice your small success? Yes? Success!

Eventually these small successes build a foundation upon which you build bigger goals to achieve more success. Successful thinking is a habit. Don't expect to graduate to the top right away. Even if you did, the odds of having the fucking skill set (ie: practice hours) under your belt to handle the pressure and workload would be small to nil, and the result would be catastrophic. Example: Trump becoming president of the United States.

Next up: money or prosperity.

Oh, for fuck's sake. God damn, son of a bitch, for fuck's sake, give me a fucking break for cryin' out loud. Money. It's all about the money, ain't it? We all fucking want money like it's the only thing worth having. I want money. I think that having money will make my life so much fucking easier but I think if I had a ton of fucking money, I'd have a new set of shitty problems that would require just as much effort and angst to manage as not having money does now. I am not loaded, despite what being a published author might have you think. No fucking way. However, that is because I have not been following my own damn advice and that is part of the reason I am writing this. I, too, need to hear this shit.

I had a moment, just a moment, a quick little "... ergh..." moment... Okay, so, remember when Totoro was waiting at the bus stop with Satsuki and she gave him her dad's umbrella because all he had was that silly little leaf and it was dripping water on his nose? And remember when he was discovering the joys of umbrellas and rainy nights and standing under rain drenched trees? And, the rain drops fell from the tall trees and landed on his umbrella and he was startled and his eyes popped open wide? Remember that? Yeah, that was me at 2am when I realized I had about $20 in my bank account and my mortgage is due...then I settled into my bed, my warm bed, and realized that there wasn't a fucking thing I could at 2am to make the situation any better, except maybe get up and write. (I didn't.) And mine wasn't a happy realization but I had the same startled look and feeling as Totoro with the raindrops.

Money is a major fucking motivator for a lot of people, in both good and bad ways. I'm not going to go so far to say that the root of all evil is money but I do think that there is too much fucking greed in our culture, in the world, and that maybe money is something that shouldn't be hoarded in vast amounts. Regardless of my take on capitalism, socialism, overpaid CEOs and college football coaches and the like, let's talk about money as a measure of success.

That's really fucking stupid.

Especially if it is your only measure of success. Imma ask you some more rhetorical questions because this is a book and I don't expect to hear your answers anyway. This is shit you need to think about and if you want one of those stupid little worksheets for the back of the book so you can feel like you are making progress on your personal growth path, then fine. I'll put one in. Just kidding, I probably won't. (You just checked the back of the book for a worksheet, didn't you?)

Rhetorical question 1: Did you get shells in your eggs? This is now my baseline question for whether or not you have done something successfully today. Did you get any fucking shells in your mother fucking eggs? Did you? No? Success.

Did your non-shelly eggs yield you any money? Meaning, did successfully making non-shelly eggs, consuming said non-shelly eggs, retrieving the energy through adequate digestion from non-shelly eggs propel you towards doing something else productive with your day that generated some revenue? Yes? Success.

It is easy to forget the basics.

After eating your non-shelly eggs, going to work or doing your work and [see above] contributing to the general goodness of your immediate area is a good baseline for success. I'm not going to go down the rabbit hole of people saying "But there are no jobs!" because I have a lot to say on that subject but let's just assume for the moment that you have a job to go to or a job to do.

Go do it.

After it is done, you should stand there for a quick tick and say to yourself, without looking around to see if anyone has noticed your presence, "I did a good fucking thing here. Yay, me." I have two kids, I rarely say "good job" to them. Instead, I say things like "solid effort, kiddo" or "you did it." This praises the work, not the outcome because outcomes can be successes or failure and failures can be just as valuable as successes.

◆ ◆ ◆

Anecdote Time!
My boy is a picky eater. He didn't eat dinner one night. After, we were sitting on the couch watching Jeopardy! He says, "How hot does the stove need to be to make an egg?" (It is always about fucking eggs around here. We eat a lot of eggs. I should get some fucking chickens! Brilliant!) I said, "Well, it is a gas stove so about 7, which is medium hot."

"Oh okay."
A few minutes go by and he says "How much butter do you use?" and I answered his question with how I make eggs, which is with a lot of fucking butter. More Jeopardy! After a tick, he gets up and wanders to the kitchen. I'm not paying too much attention. He's eight, if he fucks something up, I'll know.

He fucked something up.

He screams and then runs in really pissed off. Of course, I'm concerned for his safety so I ask him where he hurts and he said that he wasn't hurt, just scared. I said, "What are you scared of?" Again, he's eight, he knows there are no monsters and that Santa Claus is fiction. His response? "Flipping the egg." Flipping the egg? and then I put it all together. He took it upon himself to make a White Egg, which in our house is just a fried egg white. Unless its scrambled, my kids don't like the yolk yet. I get to the kitchen and on the stove is the pan I use to fry eggs. In the pan is a shit ton of butter (well done, kiddo) and an egg white without a speck of yolk or shells gently frying in the pan. He tried to flip the egg but since his face is just about 8" over the top of the stove, he was rightfully scared of hot melted butter splatter in his face. I grab the spatula that hit the floor, the best spatula we have for egg flipping, (See? They learn even when we think they aren't paying attention) wiped it off and flipped the egg. He's standing off to the side, hands wringing exactly the way my mother wrings her hands, expecting me to be mad at him for all of it. Instead, I said, "I'm proud of you for taking the initiative to cook your own egg. You did it the way I do it. You paid attention to my cooking lessons. Well played, little one."

He got all hung up on the fact that he didn't have the balls to flip the egg himself and was beating himself up over that one small 'failure' to which I responded "...but look at all the success. You cracked and separated the egg flawlessly, the butter is perfect, the pan isn't too hot, you have the right utensils and a plate at the ready. You even gathered the spices. How is this a failure?"

As his parent, it is my job to teach him how to be self-sufficient and render myself about 99.5% obsolete once he's an adult. That is a job I take very seriously. For my son, this includes teaching him how to be proud of his successes and how to think critically about his 'failures'. I don't think I will have this challenge with my daughter They couldn't be more different. He went from being angry at his own perceived inadequacies to proud that he handled a situation like cooking an egg alone. From this point on, I shouldn't have to praise him at all about cooking an egg. He has the confidence now to either try flipping the egg again on his own or asking me for help with that one step because hot butter splatter is a real thing at his height. He leveled up.

◆ ◆ ◆

Level the fuck up ... but don't get too cocky.

Praise yourself, and be happy with that level of praise, for a good day's work. The paycheck at the end of the week is good, too, but I really do believe and you should too, that the ultimate motivation for a job well done is just that: a job well done.

Flip your fucking eggs, people.

And, maybe some level of advancement for your general community. Has what you just did made someone's life better in some way, even your own? If you get the TPS reports done, or the eggs cooked with no shells, and send those down the line to the next person in the chain, will they be happy with the level of success you achieved with your part of it? Yes? Success, yo.

Do that enough and you'll probably get promoted. Usually promotions come with bigger paychecks. Just putting that out there.

Rhetorical question 2: How much money do you need to feel successful? There was a Princeton study done some years back. I'll find it and reference it so you know that I'm not pulling this little tasty tidbit right from my ass but that big brained people figured this out instead. Anyway, the study put the benchmark right around $75,000 USD. That number, 75k a year. That much money and people feel no more sense of happiness if they have or earn over that much money. You could be pulling in Warren Buffet level bones and yet feel no more happiness than the dude down the street working a 9-to-5 and pulling in about 75k. Actually, as stated before, making a ton more money might bring with it mo' problems. I'm not the first to say this.

This constant fucking quest to have more money so that you can buy shit you don't really need because marketing people or advertisers tell you you should want that, hell, that you *NEED* it, drives me insane. Think for yourself, you brain dead shit stain. Yes, I'm swearing again because this pisses me off. Don't stare at the television or your phone and see these ads and automatically think that you now have a problem that only a shoddily made piece of pollution can fix. Humans have needs and wants and I would venture a guess that 90% of the things that people say they need are actually wants. You don't need another pair of jeans. The jeans you have a perfectly fine, you *want* another pair of jeans. Unless you do actually need them for your job or something but that's besides the fucking point. The point is learning to discern your fucking desire to own and buy and compete with the next guy because you have some sort of fucked up FOMO. Keep in mind that I'm keeping this really fucking relative. If your job is to explore new tech for your company and keep your company's sales team using the latest and greatest for their jobs, then for your job, you might need to get the latest Android smartphone...but then your company should be buying that for you to explore. You, yourself, don't actually need the latest thing. Not when you don't actually have the discretionary cash to buy it. By the way, do you know the difference between discretionary income and disposable income? You should. I'm not going to go into a big long discussion about that. There are several wonderful financial planners and financial wizards out there with a wealth of resources to help you determine the difference and which one you actually have. That pun was intended.

I am also not friggin' saying that you can't go buy yourself something nice. Sure. Do that. What I am suggesting is that you really think about how much money you really need for the things that really fucking matter and really think about how you are spending that money.

Which leads me to....

Rhetorical question b: Why do you want a ton of money? Would being able to flash that much cash at people, to throw 100s around like they were 1s make others like you more? Are you that big of a prick that you think money is the answer to being a decent fucking human being? You might be thinking, "I AM a decent fucking human being and I've got exactly dick" and you'd probably be right. Maybe you are a decent fucking human being and maybe you've got exactly dick and maybe you think that if you had the opposite of "exactly dick", what, is that "exactly pussy"? I don't know. Anyway, if you think you had the opposite, then you might feel better about yourself or that people would like you more. If people don't like you, I doubt it has anything to do with your net worth, financially-speaking, of course. Maybe you're an asshole. Having money and being a nice person are not mutually exclusive. If you don't know what "mutually exclusive" means and many people don't, it means that two things cannot occur together. If something is NOT mutually exclusive, they can happen at the same time or exist at the same time. In our example, you *can* be a good person *and* have money. Having a lot of money doesn't automatically (and shouldn't) make you an asshole. If you become an asshole in the quest for a ton of money, well, then you need my other book, and this one, and someone to slap you about the head and face for a bit.

◆ ◆ ◆

Anecdote Time!
I met a young girl in a college class a few years back. I'm still toiling away at my degree, which up until recently, I didn't really need but nowadays if you don't have that piece of paper, well, then somehow you are 'less'. It was a general education class for the specific degree and so there was quite a mix of students. We were paired up and asked to interview our partner, then when the dreaded introductions came around, that no one fucking likes, we were to introduce our partner. Very fucking clever on the teacher's part, eh? Supposedly to reduce the tension and the fucking stress of having to tell people about yourself instead of just letting that shit unfold naturally.

I interviewed my partner who clearly had more important things to do with her day and her life than be in this class and certainly one of those things was not talking to me. She said her name was something, something very normal but then said "You can call me Coco Red." She seemed like a normal young woman with normal colored hair so I asked how she got the nickname. She looked up from her phone with a huge look of disdain and said "I gave that to myself. It's my stage name. I'm going to be famous." Now this shit was getting interesting. I said, "Nice. For what will you be famous?" My grammatically correct sentence structure threw her off. There was a quick look of "What the fuck...? on her face, as if to say, 'G*iii*rl, speak English.' When I saw this look of disdain and incomprehension, I said, since we were in an art class, "Are you planning on being a famous clothing designer? Or shoes? Do you sing? What is your talent? Your superpower?" I really did want to know. Maybe she was the Next Big Thing and I could say that I knew greatness before all y'all. She looked up from her phone and in a completely normal voice, with all the conviction she had which was backed by true belief, she said "I'm going to be famous for being famous," then rolled her eyes at me and went back to her phone. And you know what? That's exactly how I fucking introduced her.

◆ ◆ ◆

And to all that I say, "Fuck you, Kardashians." I kind of blame them. Seriously. I can't think back to someone or some other group of people who are literally famous for being famous and as famous as them, maybe Paris Hilton*, who I believe accidentally mentored Kim but I think it was actually the dad who was anyone who did anything in that family, both the Kardashians and the Hiltons. He was a lawyer, Robert Kardashian. Love or hate him for his lawyering; that's not my point, to argue the details or politics. My point is he had a job, a real job. Like, for reals. From what I know of the Kardashians, they are blessed with really good looks, that's a fine-looking family. The roll of the DNA dice for them has always come up 7 or 11 with that bunch. Kris is a master marketer. See? She makes you want to buy what they are selling even though what they are selling is essentially nothing. They are selling you nothing and you buying that shit up in droves. Fucking hilarious. That's America, people.

What value do they provide to the world as a whole? Not much that I can see. They are fun to watch, I guess? They have, or had, a show, Keeping Up with The Kardashians. They marry famous people and have affairs with other famous people. I'm not sure. I really haven't delved very deeply into their mythology because I don't really fucking care. My life is real. Their life, compared to my life, is fiction. Their lives do not matter in the scope of my life. Unless Kim, Kourtney, Khloe, Kendall, Kylie and Kris want to start supporting me and my family financially, I cannot care about them nor do I want to spend my time on them. My opinion on this, however, seems to be in the minority. A vast amount of people spend a considerable amount of brain power and time watching this clan (or should it be klan? Oo, no, that's worse) do whatever it is they do. They are a symptom of a disease, the Kardashians. I'm sure they are all very lovely people when the cameras are off, but what they are selling is a disease to the rest of us. They seem to make The Rest of Us want what they have and the odds of ever having that are truly very slim. So instead We All watch, and dream and gossip and pretend that We, too, could be like them.

They differ from royalty, as I understand royalty, insomuch as they don't uphold an ideal. They are merely bread and circus, the Kardashians. If you are not familiar with "bread and circuses" as a reference to a politics and culture, pick up a fucking book.

Question, really question, yourself about why you think you want a lot of money. Think long and really fucking hard about your motivations for chasing the Almighty Dollar. I am not disparaging rich people. I'm not extolling the 'virtues' of poverty because there ain't nothing glamorous about being poor. I'm not a socialist trying to undermine capitalism. I am merely asking for introspection in the desire to jump from one to the other with no set plan in place. I am merely asking you to fucking think, critically think, about what you think you want and how you plan to get it because a big part of getting your head out of your fucking ass is planting your head squarely into your true fucking reality and living attentively in it.

◆ ◆ ◆

See where I am going with this? The definition of success for any given day might be different than the day before and I know what you are thinking, you're thinking "Fuck you, EB. That's not success. That's just living your life and not being a total fucking douchebag. That's not major success. I need major success to feel worthy of anything."

Why?

Is this about the Kardashians again? Are you still believing what the ads are telling you? I'm not wearing a tin foil hat, I'm just asking some questions.

Here's another one: are you still comparing yourself to everyone else?

You silly, stupid, fucking idiot.

Don't do that. I will slap your hand. I will. Don't do that.

Don't compare.

Success is a personal thing, like Jesus. And taking a shit. This is something that you have to figure out on your own. You cannot compare your life to anyone else's in a general sense. Oh, and if you're one of those people who has to one-up everyone around you, let me be the first to tell you that no one likes that shit. No one fucking cares. You need to go back to How Not to be an Asshole and re-read chapter one. Just go. Ugh.

Really?

Where were we? Success and Jesus and dropping a deuce. These are all personal things. Things that you have to figure out on your own. Do not let anyone else tell you what success is for you, and that includes the TV or your smartphone or your mother.

*As as aside, I got to wondering what ol' Paris was up to these days (early 2018) and it seems that she's planted herself in Ibiza (*niice*) been quite busy building her businesses. Well done, Paris. Well done.

SECTION 1: VICTIM MENTALITY

> "You are responsible for your life. You can't keep blaming someone else for your dysfunction. Life really is about moving on." ~Oprah Winfrey

Everyone has someone like this in their life; the person who is always on the short end of the stick. That someone who always has it worse than you. Remember my mentioning the one-upping earlier? Well, there is one-downing, too. "Oh, you lost your job due to outsourcing? Well, I lost my job, too. Twice in one year." It's the same damn thing but in reverse; how much worse they have it than you. They are always the victim. There is always something else keeping them from doing what they need to do to be whatever their definition of success is. They are a Victim of Circumstance. They are a Victim of Others. They are a Victim of the Times. What the fuck ever. They just want to be a victim because then they can claim they have no responsibility for the outcome. If you are thinking, "Hmm, I don't think I have someone like this in my life..." then it's probably you.

Being or acting like a victim all the time is fucking exhausting to those around you. I know this firsthand because I used to play the victim all the time. I blamed one particular thing and it was my fall back. Every fucking time something went wrong or I made a boneheaded decision out of impulsiveness I would usually end up blaming something other than my shitastic decision making skills. I had a scapegoat. Every time. For me, in my head, it worked great! However, the older I got, the less it worked for me. The veneer wore thin.

The reason this is exhausting for others is because the other people see more clearly that the decision being made is not the best it could be and maybe they'll try to warn your dumb ass about it. Victims usually don't take anyone's advice, ever, but ask for it constantly and then want to complain endlessly about the shitty outcome. It's a vicious circle that will eventually cause you to lose most of your friends as the years wane on. I know this firsthand. How do I know? Because I just described myself.

I called these "steps" before like what they have you go through in Alcoholics Anonymous. AA's 12-step program is pretty well known and I am not going to be so bold as to say "it's just like that" I don't fucking know. You tell me. What I do know is that these are things that I have discovered about myself and about others and feel that they each need to be dealt with. I've created the order here in the way it makes sense to me to tackle this problem. You might feel differently about it, so jump around. Your situation might be all kinds of fucked up and in a different order, so just keep that in mind.

STEP 1: STOP BLAMING YOUR FUCKING PARENTS.

> "You can't live your life blaming your failures on your parents and what they did or didn't do for you. You're dealt the cards that you're dealt. I realized it was a waste of time to be angry at my parents and feel sorry for myself." ~ Drew Barrymore

I can feel it right now. I haven't even published this yet and I can feel the anger and fucking passion, and the deep angst just flying back at me after I wrote those words in the title of this part.

Stop fucking blaming your fucking parents.

There is some bad, bad fucking shit out there like those two fucktards in California with the 13 kids. People are fucking horrible to kids. Some of the stories of parents and the fucking shit they did to kids for any number of fucked up, disgusting reasons, it makes my stomach turn. As in, I don't want to think about that shit for too long. I have kids. I could never.... I just couldn't ever do anything like what some parents do to their kids.

Sure, I say shit out of anger, and I get frustrated and I scream or yell or get pissed. I don't hit them. I don't demean them and I sure as hell don't abuse them. The horrific shit out there... *<trails off and thinks about some of it>* I can't do it. I can't think about that. I just get too fucking pissed off.

There are three ways this goes if you are a kid of some truly fucked up parents. 1.) you rise above. 2.) become a victim and you dwell. 3.) you perpetuate their shit.
I am not even going to deal with number 3 because, again, that will just piss me off. I just can't. They're kids, people. *KIDS.*

For the sake of my own sanity writing about this part, let's go with something more mundane and probably middle of the road. Here's the gist of my story and remember, this is from my perspective and I'll go over that in a minute.

My parents separated and divorced right around the time I was 7. I'm pretty sure it was in the summertime. My bedroom window faced east and I remember the sunlight. The details are sketchy but I remember the feelings I had.

Over the next decade, it felt to me that my parents were pretty checked out when it came to me. My brother was different; had a different take on life and getting by and he was older by three years so there were some emotional and cognitive development advances he had to his advantage that I didn't possess. Three years is a lot with kids.

I remember the way their divorce *felt* more than anything. Because of who I am and how my brain is programmed (more on that, too), I felt like an inconvenience to everyone. My parents split up the kids. I lived with my mom; my brother with my dad. My mom moved to Columbus, but we were all from Cleveland originally. For visitation, someone had to come get me or take me or when no one could be bothered, my ass was thrown on a Greyhound bus for the ride to Cleveland alone. I was probably 10 years old. That felt to me like I wasn't important enough for my dad to come get me. That he couldn't make the concessions to put out the time, you know? For my mom, I think it felt like she wasn't going to go out of her way to make my dad's life easier.

As for growing up as a teen, away from my brother and dad, with just my mom who worked in sales and was gone some... It felt lonely. I was alone. I had a family but we weren't together. We weren't even friendly. The extended family took sides and it felt like I was on the losing side. To my paternal grandmother, I was a reminder of *her*, the woman who tarnished the life of her beloved oldest son. I was treated in the way my mother would have been treated and that was truly unfair. I couldn't find solace in my grandparents. My paternal grandfather was more neutral. I think, I felt, that he treated me neutrally, just like any of the other of his grandkids and because of that I felt safe with him. And, honestly, I miss him a lot. My mother's parents were all dead by this point. I had only my father's parents and one didn't like me at all and made no bones about telling me so. Even at 10-ish, I knew that I was being treated unfairly and I thought that shit was fucked up.

I've never really been one to hide from confrontation or be afraid to say what is on my mind. What has changed is my tactics in how I present myself but at that age, there was no filter and often I used bluntness as a form of defense. I attacked with my mouth, so to speak. I am little. "You're wee" as my husband calls me and so when I was a kid, even smaller and so I used my words to hurt when I was being attacked in some way.

Keep in mind that these memories and the way I felt growing up were all colored by my filters, by how my brain worked and how I interpreted things around me. As a grown woman and a parent, I try to look at my kids through the lenses that they might have, to feel things as they might feel them, to truly empathize with their point of view. I don't know how many parents do that. When my mother would tell me that what I was thinking or feeling was invalid, that fucking hurt, because to her, she didn't see the situation in the same way. I felt it. I fucking felt that shit to my fucking core and it is because of all the layers of my life built up to taint, color, mold how my brain feels things. Her invalidating my feelings was and is one of the worst things I ever felt and still sometimes feel.

These are not direct quotes but general ideas, she would say things like "Why are you crying? That's no reason to cry." Things like that. Instead of really wanting to know why I was crying because it often felt like she didn't care, and truly listening to my concerns, she would just dismiss my reason on principle because she would feel that it wasn't a valid reason for the effort of crying. Even then I would say things like "Don't compare me to you as you are right now. That's not a fair comparison" and it truly isn't. How can you compare someone to someone else who has 25 years more of life experience? That's just really fucking stupid.

My mother probably did care about why I was crying but it took years for me to truly understand that for her, emotions that are not hers, well, she just can't handle them unless they are happy emotions because those don't take any effort on her part at all. Even now, if I talk to her about anything negative or bad in my life, it has to be told in the past tense. Like, "Oh and this happened but it's all cool now. I don't need anything from you to help me handle this or how I feel about it. It's all good, but yeah, thanks." She just can't deal with any of that shit and really doesn't want to. I grew up with a sense of "I can't be bothered by your problems" from my mom. I guarantee that she would disagree with this perspective and that is totally fine. This is my filter. This is how this felt to me at the time and it was (is) something that I carried with me into adulthood and it was supported by the way my father treated me during those tumultuous formative teen years as well.

My father was less of a presence in my life than my mother was, obviously. I didn't live with him but spent a few weekends each month and a few weeks in the summer with him. My father has passed on, he's almost 9 years gone now and I miss him every day. I credit deeply my stepmother with helping turn his mental life around. I do credit her with helping me re-establish a relationship with my father after I became an adult but on different terms.

As a child, as a small human learning how to navigate the world and how to emote properly for maximum benefit in that world, we need our parents to help us manage our emotions. We, as little children, look to our parents for how they are handling situations and then we emulate them because that's what they are doing. Other children handle things differently, I know this, so remember that I am expressing all of this from *my* point of view. Your personal experience might be similar or worlds different.

I can say this: I would see how my parents would respond emotionally to each other, their respective partners and the world in general and I tried my best but it wasn't fucking good enough. What I did notice and changed was what I saw them doing with their health. I didn't take up smoking even though so many around me did. I didn't really drink alcohol and do drugs because I saw the effects and I knew I didn't want that fucking shit in my life. I just couldn't seem to do this with my life's perspective and my emotions, and I still fucking struggle with this shit, sometimes on a daily basis. It is just the way I am wired. My son is wired like me. Thankfully, I now have the tools to help him earlier than I was helped.

I needed my parents to teach me how to emote properly in the world. I needed an emotional education because that didn't come naturally to me. Seeing that smoking was a bad idea, or getting fucked up, etc.; those things were blatantly fucking obvious but I failed with the emotional stuff and thus my emotional life and how I related to other people was always kind of screwed up. I needed to go through the School of Hard Knocks and see therapists before I learned any of these lessons. I lost friends and became thoroughly lonely and desperate. I remember standing in the kitchen, feeling like I was falling inside, like my insides were imploding or falling in to a black hole and I wanted to pick up the phone, the old corded wall phone that hung in the kitchen with a cord so twisted and wrapped up but long enough to reach all the way into the living room, and call a friend; to reach out over the phone for a hand to just hold on to so that I wouldn't fall completely away and be lost inside myself. I stood there, shaking, arms wrapped around myself, deep in the feelings of the betrayal I had just experienced, or believed I experienced, and realized that there wasn't a person I could ring anymore that would take the call and talk me off the ledge. I sucked so badly at emoting well and correctly for any given situation that I had alienated people I cared about, who did care about me but were so fucking exhausted with me that they just *couldn't*, you know? They just couldn't anymore. To stand there and feel so helplessly alone was one of the worst feelings of my life. I realized that not all of these people could be so fucked up that they were the ones with the problem; not when I realized that the common denominator to all of them was me.

I could have let go. I could have let myself go and fall into that black hole of loneliness and despair. That would have been the easy choice.

Effortless.
Smooth.
Painless.

And yet, I knew as a teen where that hole would lead. It would eventually lead to drug abuse, alcoholism and probably death. Suicide ran in the family. That ledge, the one I needed talked off of, slipping off that ledge would probably have led me there.

I refused.

I stood there, in that kitchen with the breakfast nook and dated wallpaper, with the twisty corded phone and I refused. I decided that I would rather be alone than dead. What goes up must come down, right? I can't stay alone forever, right? As in the laws of physics, statistics and probability actually prove that I couldn't be alone forever. Unless I moved to a cave in the hills, I would still have some probability of not being alone in some way. I made a choice. Probably one of the best choices of my life right then that I would not slip over the edge of that black hole. No Event Horizons for me, thankyouverymuch. I chose. Right then and right there. Quietly, with no one to hear the proclamation, with no one to tell me "good job", with no one to tell me that I made the right choice, I decided that the answer was "No."

In no way does this mean that I have never stared over the edge of that abyss and looked into it since then. I have visited The Edge many times. I have sat on the ledge of The Edge and dangled my feet in to the blackness. I daydreamed about the effects of just slipping in. The ramifications of doing so would be deep and long and irreversible, so I haven't. How selfish of me anyway, in my opinion, to think about only myself and my immediate gratification of taking away the pain. I have a bumper sticker on my car that says "Pain is weakness leaving the body." [Credit goes to the USMC, and my dad who was a jarhead.] There are times that I remember this and think about the pain. Emotional pain, specifically. What is this pain telling me? Where am I weak? What needs strengthened? What changes need to be made? When I get to The Edge, I have to stand back. I look in but I stand back. I'm at The Edge for a reason, another weakness, another hole that needs not to be patched but to be fixed.

Securely.

For good.

Okay so what the fuck does all this have to do with not blaming your parents anymore? Very good question and I'm glad I asked. It means that they did what they did and whether it was their best at the time is irrelevant. As annoying as this particular fucking tidbit of wisdom is: it is what it is. I was dealt this hand in life with the parents that I had; or as some schools of thought go: I chose my parents so that my soul could learn important lessons. I like this more than the idea of chance so when deep in emotional despair, I think "What am I supposed to be learning here?"

I have three choices. Remember those from before?

Here they are again:
1.) you rise above.
2.) become a victim and you dwell.
3.) you perpetuate their shit.

I was stuck with number 2 for a while. I, in many ways, played the victim for a long time. I blamed my parents for every fucking shortcoming in my personality and character. *They* were the ones who did this to me! *They* were the ones that fucked me up. *They* are the ones to blame for every shitty thing I have ever done. My mom didn't do this or my dad didn't do that. I needed this and I needed that. Meh meh meh whine whine whine cry cry cry. That was what I said to myself every time I fucked up and I fucked up a lot. It was a story that I told myself and it got grander and more robust as the years went on. It was a fucking Ponzi scheme of emotions.

This is what I did for years, those years that are supposed to be the best ones of the younger part of your life: your 20s and early 30s. As time went on, I shed some of this slowly. I was always looking for the how. How do I just not do this anymore? Someone tell me, please?! And yet, I wouldn't have listened anyway. Remember how I said that some people constantly ask for advice, get it, never take it and then complain about the outcome? Yeah, that was me. That was how I ended up with no friends. That standing in the kitchen thing, feeling betrayed again? The thing that led me to The Edge? I had been advised, on numerous occasions, about the person who committed the betrayal and yet I did not take said advice. Now, one could argue that I needed to go through that to get to The Edge in order to make that decision and sure, I'll go along with that. Yet how do I justify all the times after that when I asked for advice and didn't take it? I can't. I wanted to be the victim because that is easier. It is just easier. Absolving yourself of responsibility is easy when you didn't know, right? How can you be at fault if you just didn't know? Bullshit. You knew. You fucking knew and you did (or didn't) do it anyway.

Shut the fuck up.

If you are a grown ass adult, you cannot blame your parents anymore. Even if they are still trying to fuck you up, you can't blame them anymore. Why? Why not when it is so easy to do? Precisely because of that reason. If you are still living at home and you are capable of not living at home, then you cannot blame them. Blame yourself. If they are horrible people and you are allowing them access to you to continue their horribleness, don't blame them. Blame yourself. Shut them out. Who gives a fuck if they are your family? If they are horrible people to you, shut them out. If you find out over the years that it was you that was horrible and you try to fix it, odds are good, maybe not great, but good that you could patch things up, especially if you atone. My point is that if they are shitty people, cut them the fuck out. They are not what you need right now. You cannot continue to expose yourself to their fucked up shit and think that things will work out for the best. If you have been doing that and it's not working, why do you think it will continue to work in the future? If you do, then you are fucking stupid.

I mean that. Seriously.

No one deserves that, not even the truly fucked up people among us. No one deserves that so stop subjecting yourself to it and make a change.

If you choose option number 1, to rise above, then you really have to do that. You have to remove the influence. At thirty-five years old, I found a reason to move to Los Angeles; between the thought and the moving was less than two months. I fucking moved to LA. I found out later that my mother was pissed, like *pissed* that I moved. She was pissed at me the whole time I was gone, almost 4 years. I was 35, a grown woman, I could do what I wanted. My dad was startled and concerned but didn't stop me, wished me well and said he was going to be nervous for me. I get that he was nervous but he didn't guilt me. Cutting that cord and moving 2,500 miles away from the influences that shaped who I was as an adult was fucking critical to my personal growth. I do not think that I would be the same woman now if I hadn't moved away. The whole story of moving and the hot water I got myself into at first is a story for later but suffice it to say that I truly found out what I was made of in doing that move and venturing off to the Golden Coast. I fucking loved it there and I miss it so much. There are things I don't miss but I do miss what California meant to me, how it changed me, the people I met, the acceptance I felt, the growth I experienced, the fortitude and resolve I acquired. Those years were my 'college years'. I didn't go to university right out of high school. I didn't have that experience but moving to LA and living there, with four other people, communally, as a group and experiencing that time of my life... Oh, it was necessary and the best. I will definitely encourage my children to fly the coop in a big way when they are of age.

If you rise above, many times it will require cutting the cord, having distance and time. For some that means total estrangement. If you feel that this is critical for your mental health and wellbeing, for personal growth and achievements, then you should do it. Even if its just for a little while. Create the boundary. Draw the line in the sand. I remember the first time I did that with my mother. I said something like "Money and men, Mom. These topics are now off limits unless I bring them up. I just will not discuss these with you anymore." (The funny thing? My mother introduced me to my husband in a roundabout way. Ha! Irony!!)

I'm not suggesting that you put up impenetrable walls but maybe you should if you're one of those kids that experienced truly horrific acts. Do it. Save yourself. If your situation is a little more like mine, with parents that maybe didn't do the best job they could have but tried their best with what they had at the time, then boundaries need to be set and you need to stick to them. What you can't do is blame them. Not anymore. That shit has to stop right the fuck now. That's over. It's done. You're an adult and now this shit is up to you.

Suck it up, buttercup.

I'm serious.

Just fucking stop.

Rise above.

Be better.

And, yeah, it's a choice. Just choose it.

> "If you hate your parents, the man or the establishment, don't show them up by getting wasted and wrapping your car around a tree. If you really want to rebel against your parents, out-learn them, outlive them and know more than they do.' ~Henry Rollins

STEP 2: STOP BLAMING EVERYONE ELSE AND LOOK IN THE MIRROR, DICKHEAD

> "It is always easy to blame others. You can spend your entire life blaming the world, but your successes and failures are entirely your own responsibility." ~ Paulo Coelho

We've established that you should no longer be blaming your parents for anything. Special circumstances do exist but this isn't about that. We're talking run-of-the-mill shit, every day "happens all the time" kinda shit. Being a victim means that you find any and all reasons to not be responsible for the shit that is happening to you. In being said victim, you must find other reasons why the world is so horribly unfair to you and that means finding other things to blame. What I'd like you to do right now is get up and find a place with a mirror. Look in it. See that person? That's who you blame. That face looking back at you. Let me clarify: that face should be yours. If you see some fucked up ghost or apparition, then that's a whole other situation. I suggest running. Away. Fast. Then burn the fucking house down. Actually, no. Don't do that but do run away.

Ain't nobody got time for that shit.

Fuck you, ghost.

If you have no ghost in your mirror freaking your ass out, then take a good long look and have a fucking gander at the person you should be blaming.

Everyone else in your life, in some capacity, is mostly blameless. What I mean by this is that some women out there will say, "I can't leave. He'll kill me" or "He'll hurt the kids" or any other combination of this stuff. I'll be gentle here because I *know*. Maybe not with someone who would pull a real trigger but definitely with someone who wanted nothing more than to make me hurt. Hurt me indiscriminately because it was fucking fun for him. Watch me disappear, watch me panic, watch me do any number of things and then tell me how fucked up I was for doing it. It was a no-win situation and maybe it is not someone who is doing any of these things like threatening your life or the life of your children but just enjoys not being a good person, you know, they are an asshole.

Let me back the fuck up. I dated a guy in high school and that spilled over to dating him off and on out of high school and on and on. It was really quite tiring for my friends to hear "Oh, you're back with him? Again?" and then they'd mutter under their breath, "When will she fucking learn?" Because I hadn't. Remember that story earlier about being alone in my kitchen and shaking from the fact that I had just been betrayed and that I had no one to call to talk me off the ledge? Yeah, that was him...but I let this shit go on for years and years and years. I will include an addendum to this story that I wrote in a future letter to my kids. The letter is about that situation and why it was so fucked up and what to do about it.

Things didn't change for me with that particular guy until I got betrayed again by him and a close friend. Here's the anecdote and keep in mind that this story is from my perspective with a lifetime of filters in front of my vision, some of those filters are clear and maybe some not so much.

◆ ◆ ◆

Anecdote Time!
I was living in German Village, which is a historic district in Columbus, Ohio, so I would have been in my early thirties and yes, I was back with him. Again. There had been more proclamations of personal change and professions of him really wanting to be with me and that I was The One and all that fucking shit. Let's call him Monroe and the other party to this mess, Fucking Bitch. Oh, no. That won't work. Let's call her Betty.

Betty and I were friends from the neighborhood, having met through other friends I met at the informal dog park that exists at Schiller Park. There's a lot of back story here so I'll just hit the high points because I know you all want to get to the juicy stuff and why I call her Fucking Bitch in my head, even to this day.

Right.

At some point in our friendship, Betty got breast implants. She went from a lovely rack that was a wholesome B-cup (C'mon, everyone loves boobs) to D-cups, I think. I was quite astounded because I thought her tits were lovely to start with and would have loved to have had what she had naturally. Let's not dwell on the titties, shall we? She's divorced and stacked and is enjoying using her Girls to flirt and flaunt and relive her 20s. Being married in her twenties kept her from doing these things then so she was doing them in her early 30s with new boobs. A year or so before the event that led to me calling her Fucking Bitch in my head and sometimes out loud, we went to a bachelorette party for a mutual friend up on Kelley's Island. For those of you who are unaware of the state of Ohio as nothing more than potentially being full of cows, corn and not worthy of your time other than to fly over it, we have several islands in Lake Erie. Check out Kelley's Island, South Bass Island, Put-in-Bay area of Middle Bass, Gibraltar Island. There's a whole bunch of 'em. These are great places to visit in the summer and can feel like a world away when you live in Ohio and can't really get to a saltwater beach or anything. It can be quite lovely. We camped as kids up there with my dad. His old partner from the police force (my dad was a cop) had a B&B that we would visit sometimes, too. Anyway, we went to the islands for girls only bachelorette party and shenanigans ensued. Good times were had by all.

On the way back from that, Betty was driving us in her convertible, the sun was shining, the weather was glorious and it was a good time of my life to be single and reasonably attractive; we were discussing men and such and she said something along the lines of "You just don't mess with your girls' guys" meaning that the men involved with your friends are just off limits. Always. Unless you get permission. This seems fairly fucking decent, right? Like, if you are a decent fucking human being who isn't a selfish fucking asshole, then this should be a fucking no-brainer...right?

Sure, when it applies to everyone but you.

After she got her new tits and I was back with Monroe, she decided that he was her next target. I don't remember all the details of the day but she was at my place, dressed in 'work around the house' wear and I had mentioned that he was coming over to pick me up and that we were going to go grab a bite to eat. She took her leave then called me and said she had to drop something off at my place, or whatever, it was all just a fucking ruse; and when she came back over...and Monroe was now there...she was dressed in short shorts that Daisy Duke would have been embarrassed to wear and a top so tight and low cut that it seemed pointless. Monroe and I sort of stared. I mean, how could you not? Those tits were so fucking big, first of all, and way too high up, and gravity defying. It was difficult not to look at them even when they were not on such obvious display. I guess that was totally the point of buying the fucking things in the first place. She was peacocking all over my guy. In front of me. Like a Fucking Bitch.

Fast forward.

I make stupid mistakes, like keeping both of those twats in my life, and I'm home sick with another bout of ovarian cysts. (Side note: for me, they went away and didn't come back after I gave up drinking soda every day. Just putting that out there.) I'm in pain, I have a fever, I feel like fucking shit but I'm at my desk working through all of it because: self-employed. Monroe is there "taking care of me" which he fucking didn't know how to do, and Fucking Bitch calls me in tears and she needs my help. I said that I couldn't help her because I was sick but asked what the problem was and she said she is locked out of her shed. Monroe offers to help her open it and leaves. He's gone for hours. Multiple. More than one. Fucking Bitch lived down the street, only a mile away. What the fuck is taking so long? That Fucking Bitch and that stupid fucking man.

◆ ◆ ◆

I'm ending the story here because I just get so fucking pissed off at myself for allowing the situation to happen because I didn't have the fucking backbone to tell both of them to piss the fuck off...and I'm not someone who shies away from confrontation.

By telling both of them to piss the fuck off, I would have been lonelier. Less people in my life. I have known Monroe since I was fifteen and now, at my current age, I truly believe that if you've known someone since birth, it doesn't fucking matter. If they are a horrible person, then you get rid of them. I was in that shitty situation because I allowed it. I allowed them to be my friend and significant other, respectively. Neither one of them really cared about how I felt about the situation and if they were truly my friend and my partner, then they would have. They would have had some fucking respect but neither of them did. Neither of them fucking cared about anything but getting hands on some giant gross-ass tits and dicks in slots. That was it and fuck all to the people who get hurt along the way. Monroe probably thought, "I've done this in the past with no major repercussions. She always comes back so sure, I'll dip my wick." And Fucking Bitch probably thought "She won't even know."

I fucking knew.

If you even suspect something is going on, if your gut is fucking firing up like the God damn Fourth of July, then there is probably something going on. Cut that shit loose. It's happening and there is no fixing it. Not in my book. You make that call for yourself. I cannot and will not tell you what to do but let me tell you this: If you stay and that shit keeps happening over and over, who do you think is to blame? Not Fucking Bitch. She showed her true colors. And, not your version of That Fucking Man. He has shown his colors, too. Cut them the fuck loose. Walk away and don't look back. You don't owe people like that anything. I don't even owe them this fucking anecdote or the energy of my anger and yet it is the perfect example of having only myself to blame.

Years later, Fucking Bitch hit me up over social media. My antennae went up as if to say, "Huh? What the fuck do you want from me now?" I was on high alert. She'd only taken from me, given nothing and I'm sure she wasn't about to start now. She wanted me to lie; to change the truth so that it would reflect back on her as her being better than she actually was in hopes of getting a job doing something she probably wasn't qualified for. I said "No, and don't call me again."

Bridge: burnt.

And most importantly, I don't give a fuck what she is doing now. I don't fucking care. Not my problem. I can't care. If I care about her and her bullshit, the odds are I will get hurt again in some way. She might move in on my guy just because she feels she can and nothing more, leaving yet another wake of destruction in her path. It's about satisfying a fucking impulse, a desire, a conquest. It's not about love. It rarely ever is. It is about hurting people while making yourself feel better and if that's you, then you are a fucking asshole.

Here's the deal with The Fucking Man, the man I've named Monroe in this scenario. He still, even now, has a small pull. Fucking Bitch? Don't care. Monroe? There's still a little twitch. Why the fuck is that? I wrote about this in a letter to my kids, a letter they will get later. I write these things now so that I don't forget them with the hopes that I won't fucking forget to give them the information when they are older.

I'll share this all with you because it is fucking key. I will apologize now for the lack of profanity. There is some but not as much. Names have been changed to protect the guilty.

> There's something specific that I want to talk about today. It is the idea of the "Thing". I will try to be as clear as possible. Sometimes there is a Thing. This Thing could be a person or an event. And while it was happening, there were some good parts and there were some bad parts...and maybe the bad parts lead to other Things that weren't so good. The good parts of the Thing ("Thing" used here to represent anything, person or event) are what seem to stick in your mind more than the bad parts. This is an anomaly for people like you and me and maybe your sister because most people tend to remember the bad more than the good. If you remember the bad more than the good, then you'd be less likely to do that Thing again and therefore avoid more disappointment, pain, regret, what have you. But then there are people like me. There are others. We remember the good and not always the bad. When we remember the good only from a bad Thing, then we will romanticize it. We think, then, that that Thing was the best Thing ever and if only I could have that Thing again, which is how we end up going back to bad relationships because we only remembered the good and not the bad. We fantasize about how good the good was and that we want

that again. But how good was the good really? I mean, how do we know that the good that we thought was so good was really all that good in the first place? How can we trust ourselves to be objective assessors of the reality/good of the situation when, in fact, we are no longer involved with that Thing for a reason? Probably because the good wasn't all that good and the bad was really bad.

For example: Monroe. Monroe was my high school sweetheart. Our relationship was tumultuous and not always pleasant. There was lying and cheating and running around. There was dissatisfaction on both sides and yet we kept coming back to each other. Was this because when it was good, it was really good or is it because we were young and stupid and were still trying to figure out what was 'good' and what was 'bad' and our individual tolerance for both? Could be all of that but what I do remember and still sometimes feel is the IDEA of the good from that relationship. When it was good with Monroe, I felt great. I was happy. I felt loved and cared for and all that shit. He wasn't that great at providing what I needed and when he went off and did things contrary to what I needed, I felt bad. I tend not to remember those parts. I do remember them, I mean, but they are segmented and pushed away. They are Other. I remember them but they are Other and they do not have a place of importance in my life. Not like they should. I should remember that Other more than the idealized good that I felt because that was the more real part. That was the True part.
It has taken me years to realize why I end up making what would be considered to be very bad decisions and it is because I am usually thinking only about the romanticized version of the Thing.

Another example: Jenna. As you probably know, Jenna was a dog. In my mind, the best dog ever. She was a German Shepherd dog that I acquired rather abruptly. I didn't want a dog at the time and yet I ended up with her. What I remember the most about her is the good Thing. She was a good dog. She was the best dog but only because I worked very hard to make her that way. She would dig in the trash when she was bored despite knowing and being trained not to. She would still chase cats if they were outside despite being trained not to. She SHED like a mother fucker. I remember laying down with her on the floor on a particularly hot summer day. She was hot and I was laying with her, sweating. I said, "When you are gone, I will miss you so much (and that was/is true) but I will not miss your fur." That was also true. That is the Other that I tend to not remember as much, same as with her bad characteristics. In my mind, Jenna is, was, always will be the best dog ever. I sometimes want that Thing, another Jenna. I want what I felt when Jenna was alive and she was good and right. I want to feel that but what I forget is the amount of work that it took for me to train a very wild, very undisciplined dog into the amazing beast that she became. She has been dead for almost 11 years and yet it feels like it was yesterday when she died in my arms.

The tears flow so much faster for Jenna than they ever did for Monroe. Monroe hurt me in ways that Jenna never did. Sure, Jenna was frustrating at times but there was a difference in what I got from each of them. Jenna's Thing was more True and less Other. Monroe's Thing was a whole lot of Other.

As I've gotten older, I've been able to recognize more easily when I am thinking only about the Thing and not the Other. I see in myself that I am romanticizing the Idea of the Thing. I'm almost 47 years old. I was fantasizing about a third baby...because BABIES! There is so much Other about babies but they have a pretty good Thing going, too. Your Dad and I have not been being careful and there have been a few scares and while I am waiting to see if I am pregnant, I am thinking about the Thing and I am not thinking about the Other. Then, I think about the Other and I realize that for as much as I would love another baby as much as I love you and your sister, I cannot do that Thing. I cannot go down that path again. I love babies and all that they are but they cost time, money, emotion, etc. I need to be done and focus now on living to 100, at least, so that I can meet my grandchildren and actually be able to interact with them. I need to focus on working and earning and saving. I need to remember that [another child] puts a demand on the Earth that the Earth cannot sustain. Two of you is fine, my own selfish desires for the Thing and conveniently forgetting about the Other is no good.

There is another thing (lower case t) called The Pollyanna Principle. That's basically what I just described. The Pollyanna Principle is based off of a book about a girl who is an eternal optimist. This is always looking on the bright side of things, even bad things. This isn't always a bad thing to do but I think it also needs to be tempered with realism and the Other. Also along these lines is the Hedonistic Treadmill. Maybe if I gave an example, it would help.

My mother and Steve are two people who I've noticed don't like negative emotions in anyone. I'm not saying that I go out of my way to be around negative or nasty people but I do know that people have these emotions and as long as they are not abusive, it is totally fine. However, there are people out there who don't feel this way. They cannot tolerate or deal with any negative emotions of anyone around them. This makes me think that they are unable to deal with their own negative emotions and therefore project that on to others. My mother was always trying to squash my emotions that were not jubilant because she couldn't handle it. It felt to me that I was always supposed to maintain some completely unrealistic level of happiness all the time when I was around her. There can be no distress of any kind, which is funny because I think she is in a ton of distress all the time. So, growing up, I wasn't allowed to really have any negative emotions. Crying was dismissed. Anger was met with her anger when I was feeling it. Her anger was fine, mine was not. Whatever my problems were, they were not of any concern to her. As a child, I should have been able to look to my parents to help me modify and regulate my emotions into something healthy. Well, that didn't happen so I spent a good portion of my adult life learning how to "feel" and what emotions were appropriate and when. This took a lot of trial and error; relationships and jobs were destroyed along the way. Bridges were burned. That is too bad but when you have people as your parents who do not have a handle on their own emotions, where do you turn?

I was called a Pollyanna by my mother on more than one occasion. I guess I didn't understand what that meant fully or if I did, didn't see what was so bad. Now, looking back over several decades, I think it was a mechanism I used to not feel so hopeless. If I always thought and felt that things could only get better, then there was hope. Hope is what keeps us alive and going. As I get older, I still have hope but now I have tempered it with more knowledge about what realistic hope is and what I need to do to move forward effectively. I still see and feel myself getting distracted by all the shiny things and I really do need to not be diverted. There is a lot to do but it all needs to be focused on specific things that are all about the Thing and not the Other but still keeping the realistic Other available for reference so that I don't go down another fruitless path.

Seeking out mentors is also key. Even if they are just reference points that you found and you don't speak to these people personally, they should be available for reference at any time to keep you on the Straight and Narrow. Finding mentors that are willing to talk with you and help guide you is better than not, but I understand if they are not always available. Having grown up in an environment where asking for help usually meant my hand got slapped back, I didn't really seek out mentors because I felt that they would just say no anyway. For me, with you, finding that fine line between being available to help you and also just letting you figure things out on your own...it is tricky. You need to feel confident that you are capable but I also don't want to have you feel like I've left you hanging. There was a string of posts on FB that asked," At what point does it go from encouragement to enabling?" and I wrote, "when the encouragee won't try anything without the encourager present." If you constantly need me by your side, holding your hand so to speak, then I am no longer helping you be the best You possible. I am only enabling your dependence on me. My goal is not that. My goal is to provide you with the resources you need to step out into the world as a fully functioning, responsible and intelligent adult capable of navigating the world with me watching from the sidelines. I don't want to do to you what my parents did to me, which was leave me to figure out the vast majority of this on my own and then try to make me feel bad for not achieving some preconceived goal that they had of what I could do. Talk about being set up to fail. Fuck me.

Being smart isn't enough. You have to have a good command of your emotions and know how to emote properly and when. Having emotions is totally okay. I completely support you and your sister having emotions, all of them. They are all fine. They just need to be guided and controlled in certain circumstances. Good and bad emotions. We also need to learn how to not let our emotions make all the decisions because the emotions want to be in control of thinking about the Thing and not the Other. We shouldn't obsess about the Other but we should be aware of it and give it its due time. It needs to be acknowledged for what it is. I saw Monroe on the freeway. He was in his work truck and he recognized my car. I was taking [your sister] to daycare for the day. He honked and waved at me and I realized who it was. I had a pleasant feeling the rest of the day and I ended up thinking about him more than I usually do, which isn't often. I found myself only thinking of the Thing, the Idea of him that was so great. There were things that were different from how Steve is and I had to stop myself from going down that path. I could very easily ruin my relationship with Steve by pursuing the Thing in another person without remembering the Other and why I am no longer with that person now. The thoughts of him have faded as I forced myself to think about the Other more than the Thing. Crisis averted. Bad Decision avoided. Yay, me, but it is something I should have been doing 25 years ago.

My hope is that you learn this sooner rather than later. It did me no good to do this for most of my adult life and only created strife where none needed to be. I would ask advice of people and that advice they would give would be perfectly fine but I wouldn't take it because I wasn't thinking about the Other, I was only thinking about the Thing. The Thing that wasn't True. When their advice didn't fit in with my version of the Other and the Thing, then I wasn't really wanting to follow it. This frustrates people. Asking for advice from someone implies that there is a part of you that should actually follow it or at least do something different than what you are already doing. By not following the advice or even a part of it, it implies that you really don't want advice and just want to complain about things. No one really likes that. Friends are there for you but if you always just complain and never fix anything because you just focus on the Thing and not the Other then seriously can't figure out why your shit's fucked, well, then people will just wander away from you. That's no good.

If you find yourself thinking and romanticizing the Thing and not saying focused on the Other, then you only have yourself to blame. Get your head out of the clouds or the sand and look at reality. Stay focused on reality.

That was just about relationships. What about your money or your job or your major in school? What about all those other areas of your life where you are maybe focused on the Thing or the Other too much and are basing all of your decisions on some romanticized version of the Truth?
Stop it.

The bottom line to all of this is that you have to turn your focus around. Take that piercing ability to see the deficits in everyone around you on yourself. Look long, deep and hard at all the issues that you are dealing with that you think someone else is to blame. I'll betcha that *you* are the one to blame for it all.

> "A person who blames others has not begun their lesson.
> A person who blames themselves has begun their lesson.
> A person who blames no one has finished their lesson."
> ~Unknown

STEP 3: BEING DEPRESSED: FIND A WAY TO STOP THAT SHIT.

> "Depression is living in a body that fights to survive with a mind that tries to die." ~Unknown

Depression is a real thing. It ain't no joke. I think for some people, it is just a mild "I feel bad about my life and myself and shit ain't going right" kind of feeling and then for others, like me, it feels a little like being fucking trapped.

Hey, did you see the movie "Get Out"? I won't give any spoilers but for those who have, remember The Sunken Place? Yeah. It's like that. As in, I *know* that I shouldn't be feeling this way but despite my best efforts, I still do.

For those of you who haven't seen the movie and feel that this section may not apply to you, being depressed is something that you can be hyper-aware of and yet feel like you can do nothing about. If you have never felt depressed in your entire life, that's fucking awesome. I think you are in the minority. Like, fucking hard-core minority.

I'm not a doctor or an expert on depression and other mental illnesses so I can only speak from my own personal experience with it. The first thing I'd like to mention is that I think that it's really fucking unfair how much stigma is attached to a person when they say that they have been depressed or have struggled with mental illness. I think our culture suffers for that. People struggle, ya know, and that's the time we should be lifting them up, collectively, not slamming our boots on their throats and screaming, "...and fucking stay down!" Because of this, I think so many are not willing to ask for help with this issue because they are afraid of exactly that: of being stigmatized, ostracized or discriminated against for needing a little extra support. That shit's fucked up.

Let me be one to stand in front and say that I have struggled with this most of my life, in some level of intensity or another. There are days that I feel bad, that I'm overwhelmed or just stressed, like right the fuck now. Just got a robocall that the schools are closed again. Why? Something stupid like 10" of snow or some shit. Fucking lightweights. This is stressing me out. I have an 80 minute lecture to sit through and then was planning on sitting in an editing suite for another three hours to finish my project for school. Did I mention that I'm working on a Bachelor's degree? I think I did. But no. Now I have to manage the children. FML.

This is not depression. This is also me not being a victim. This is being hellaciously inconvenienced by snow and school closings and such. For me, depression has been when I stop taking physical care of myself. I don't shower, I don't eat. I lay around the house and just sort of exist without actually doing anything. Anyone who knows me well knows that I rarely lay around the house. While in this malaise, I will wander to The Edge and think about it. I look in but I don't go in. I'm cognizant enough to know the difference. The Edge of The Abyss is a scary place but The Abyss is a one way trip I have no desire to take but I look at the map.

Whenever I think about The Abyss, it has always been rather self-indulgent. This may not be the case for everyone else and I get that. Remember, that I can only speak from my own personal experience and I hope that some of it resonates with you. I do not mean to imply that this is the way it is for everyone. When I think of that, The Abyss, I only think about my own pain and taking it away. To me, that seems selfish. I have responsibilities. I have animals, kids, a husband, a house, a business, plants, etcetera. Maybe that all seems rather stupid as a reason to not die but I was raised with a very intense sense of duty. It's not just *me*, ya know? Others would be affected and I wouldn't want to be responsible for that level of pain. Those were always my reasons for backing away slowly from The Edge: whatever pain I am feeling that has brought me here could only pale in comparison to the pain I would cause by slipping over The Edge.

I think that because I was raised in a house with an intense work ethic and sense of duty to the whole, that I cannot take my own life. Doesn't mean the thought hasn't crossed my mind but for me, remember, it is an indulgent thought. "***I*** hurt. ***I*** want it to stop. Make it *stop*."

Crybaby.

Yeah, I said it but I said it about myself. I don't consider myself a 'snowflake' anymore. I used to be. Every slight upset me. Now? I don't give a fuck. I can't afford to. I take very few things said to me personally because I know that some times what someone is saying is usually more of a reflection of themselves than of me. I just happen to be a convenient place for them to dump their shit.

◆ ◆ ◆

Anecdote time!
My son was conceived in California and has a different father than my daughter. Let's call this person Kent. Kent was very upset when he found out I was pregnant, which I can understand. I didn't intend to become pregnant. My relationship with Kent was a fling in my mind; a fun way to pass the time. I got pregnant and I wasn't trying to.

Needless to say, young Kent, who was 14.5 years my junior didn't want to be a father and said as much. I won't go into too much detail as it's a Classic American Tale of a man feeling privileged and put-upon and so running away from any responsibility at all. Things happened, there were some terse discussions, meeting of the parents, (I'd only dated Kent for 6 weeks), judgments being made, etc. Kent was a Golden-Haired Boy: he could do no wrong so, of course, I must be trying to trap him.

Uh-huh. R*iii*ght.

Who tries to trap a 23-year-old with zero assets other than a gorgeous face and a hot body? I was 37 at the time. If I was going to trap a man, it would have been decades earlier and with someone who actually *had* something worth trapping. Besides, I ain't that kinda girl. (See above reference to work ethic and sense of duty.) I'd also like to add right here that I was not being a cougar. *He* flirted with *me*. When he did it the first time, I sort of grinned but then immediately assumed that there was some gorgeous, tall, west coast beauty with long hair and big boobs standing right behind me that was who he was really flirting with. It is like those scenes in movies where the main protagonist is an everyday kinda woman, average in looks but wholly underestimated in every way, who ends up with the prize... Kent was a "prize". Kent worked at a coffee shop I frequented. This wasn't a scene in a Hollywood movie: He *was* actually flirting with me and I was single so I ran with it.

Anyway, during a phone call, he accuses me of sleeping around and demands a paternity test before I moved back to Ohio, where I was planning on raising the baby. I just laughed. He didn't know that I'd had a conversation with another girl, who I was friendly with, that accidentally let it slip that she didn't think he was that good of a lay and when I inquired further, it turns out that their half-drunken romp took place while he was seeing me. And, I knew that he was interested in and probably banging the young woman he knew from one of his classes, that he eventually married, as well. Side note: the two women mentioned were not the same woman so...that makes three different women in the same span of time and he accuses *me* of sleeping around? Boy, that's rich.

◆ ◆ ◆

The point of that tidbit was that the things he was accusing me of were actually the things he was doing. He was projecting. That's the technical term for it, I think. According to Urban Dictionary, yeah...that's what he was doing. He was guilty of the action and so to not feel bad about that, he said it was me doing that to him. He was playing a victim to the situation, that I'd done something *to* him when he was an equal party to the conception. During one late night phone call that was after a text of him canceling us meeting to talk about the situation, he assumed I'd be asleep when actually I was up with the flu and morning sickness at the same time, he declared that I had no respect at all for his career and that I was ruining it. Again, I laughed. *His* career? The modeling and acting career that he barely had? I was ruining it with the baby? What about *my* career? The one I'd moved across the country to pursue? It was over as far as I was concerned but I was okay with that. He showed no interest in or empathy for my situation at all. All he thought about was himself. He wanted me to abort the baby. When I found myself in that position, pregnant at the ripe age of 37, I decided that I couldn't terminate the pregnancy to satisfy the self-centered blatherings of an immature young man.

As of this writing, it is 2018 and I am the mother to a delightful almost 9-year old boy who was and is worth every fucking sacrifice. Yes, he's challenging, isn't that the nature of kids?, but I wouldn't go back and change anything. Well, I would change not having such a stressful pregnancy. I would change that somehow but I wouldn't give him up for the world and when I am deep in my delight for my child or down in the trenches with him, I can't help but think back to the producing career I could have had, by what I could have been if I had chosen to remain childless. If I did proceed with a safe and legal abortion, it would have been for *me*, not Kent.

Let me interject here that I firmly believe in a woman's right to choose and that every woman in the **world** has a right to affordable health care for themselves and their children. I would not presume to push my beliefs on any other woman. If you are pro-life, then you need to be pro-the whole life, and not just pro-birth. Let me also state that before I had a child, I made good money. Enough to live nicely as a single person. After, not so much. My income plummeted about 75% for a variety of reasons, many of them directly related to the fact that I now had a child. I have been fighting an uphill battle ever since to get back to that level of income but our world (crediting someone on Twitter who said this:) wants women to work like they have no child and to the parent like they have no job. That is succinct enough for me to leave that statement to speak to exactly how I feel.

◆ ◆ ◆

Well, I think we all went a little tangential there, didn't we?

Back to the point: If you are depressed or others think you are depressed, then you need to seek out the solution that works best for you. Don't project your bullshit on to others and make them the reason you feel badly. Don't point your fingers at others.

You'll need to consult with your doctor(s) and be open and honest about it. Take the responsibility that there is something wrong then set about the diligent work of fixing it. For me, I spent a lot of time in cognitive talk therapy learning how to emote properly. I learned how not to be so thin-skinned and I took some SSRIs. These are a class of drugs that modify your serotonin levels. I had moderate success with them but found the side effects worse than being depressed.

I think what helped overall was going through the training of how to emote and how to relate to people in a better manner. Then, I could work with awareness with what I was thinking or feeling at any given time. Sometimes there was the sensation that things just got away from me; emotions or thoughts. Before I knew it, I was depressed or angry or wallowing in some pit of despair. The difference is that I was meta about it.

I *knew.*

I knew that's where I was and decided to set parameters for it. I would allow myself to feel shitty and have a pity party for one day. Eat all the chocolate, drink lots of sugary tea, lounge about and moan, or any other indulgent activity and then by the next morning, no matter how shitty I still felt, it was time to get my ass back in gear. I did not allow myself to stay there even if getting out of The Abyss felt like trying to climb up a steep muddy hill: one step forward, two steps back. I kept in my mind that the laws of physics state that it can't stay this way forever. Something will change, eventually, but that I have to be an active participant.

If you feel shitty, reach out to someone. Maybe your friends are tired of your shittiness. Mine were. That's fine. Find someone else. A professional. You have to do this.

This is no longer an excuse.

Today, I do not take any medications for anything. I no longer consume a daily SSRI pill to help with my emotions. Through a lot of trial and error, somewhat inspired by Tim Ferriss, I have learned that my diet drastically affects my emotions and that if I slip even a little, there will be some horrible repercussions. This may or may not be the way you are, too. You'll have to walk that path on your own and at your own pace. I did the work. I read the research. I tried different things. For me, having healthy relationships, being able to make better decisions even when under duress, and working towards some sort of career stability was more important than anything else. And when I had my kid, it became paramount. I was willing to sacrifice certain foods that I literally can never eat again in order to have a stable mind to function in all areas of my life.

I slipped the other day. The damage was huge. I almost dropped out of school on an impulse just because I fucked something up. The ramifications of that would have been long-lasting. Disastrous. I realized it was the food I had eaten and that the offending ingredient must have slipped in. I thought, "I'll wait this out." Within about 15 hours, the feelings of doom and despair started to lift but in the mean time I made no major decisions. Maybe it's psychosomatic, you say. Maybe it is. Maybe it's Schröedinger's Cat all over again: the act of merely observing the situation changed it.

I'll tell you this: I cannot force myself to feel depression, anxiety or panic. I'm not that good of an actor. What I mean by that is this: I truly think that the negative state of depression for me is exacerbated by specific foods, which are, sadly, ubiquitous. I cannot falsely maintain the feelings of depression, anxiety and panic when I don't actually feel them.

From this discovery, I no longer have the excuse of "I'm depressed" for any of my life's shortcomings. That is no longer an excuse for me and it shouldn't be an excuse for you.

If you feel depressed, anxious or panicky and this is a regular occurrence, then seek help. From someone. From somewhere. I don't know all the details of anyone's situation but I know that resources exist and you have to constantly and endlessly advocate for your fucking self. No one else will.

I also totally get that there are times when you just *can't*. I know that. I get it. I've been there. The real trick is to remember that when you *are* unstuck and actively pursue finding resources for yourself for the next time that happens. I guess what I'm saying is, is that if you know you get depressed, have anxiety or panic attacks or any other thing that keeps you from moving forward in your life, you have to actively pursue finding a way to eliminate it, manage it, control it. You won't move forward until you do.

Again, this comes down to doing the work. If you want to succeed at whatever it is you desire, you have to get your own house in order first and that includes your mental state. It's not all "out there", every bit of it is "in here".

Get your head right.

I mean that in the most gentle and kind way.

You have to.

Your life depends on it.

> From the film Italian Job (2003)
> John Bridger: "How do you feel?"
> Charlie Croker: "Fine."
> John: "Fine? You know what fine stands for, don´t you?"
> Charlie: "Yeah, unfortunately."
> Together: "Freaked-out, insecure, neurotic and emotional."

STEP 4: STOP TAKING EVERYTHING SO FUCKING PERSONALLY

> *"Don't take anything personally. Nothing others do is because of you. What others say and do is a projection of their own reality, their own dream. When you are immune to the opinions and actions of others, you won't be the victim of needless suffering."* ~Don Miguel Ruiz

I could write a whole other book about this because this was me. I took everything, and I mean *everything*, personally. Every little comment made near me or to me I found a way to make it personal and then I would lash out. Others would back away slowly from this attack and wonder what the fuck was wrong with me. This kind of behavior made it very difficult to make friends, keep friends and pursue any sort of meaningful work. I couldn't take constructive criticism because to me, it was all negative criticism. I stopped hearing the good stuff and only focused on the bad stuff.

My tendency was to remember only the good when other people were fucking me over and only remember the bad when it came to myself.

Taking things so fucking personally falls under the victim mentality section because if you do this, then you are saying that everyone around you is the reason you are the way you are. Everyone else is being mean to you. Everyone else is always putting you down. Everyone else is keeping you from being better. Everyone else is always telling you that you are wrong. That's shifting blame on to someone else, plain and simple. And, yeah, the fucking "always" and "never" bullshit. Fuck that. We'll come back to it.

Remember back in school, or even work last week, when you'd walk into a room or the cafeteria or something and people would look up at you and maybe their facial expression would shift? Did you automatically think that they were thinking about you? If you did, and maybe they were, did it ruin the rest of your day because you just assumed they were thinking something horrible? More than likely, they weren't or maybe they were thinking "cute shoes" and then their thoughts turned to how they can't afford your cute shoes because they have no money and that thought shows up on their face and you think the scowl is about you personally when it is not but you interpret the scowl to mean they hate your fucking guts when really they hate the fact that they have no money to buy the cute shoes you're wearing.

If you are completely unable to hear what someone else has to say about anything that has to do with you because you automatically assume that everything is going to be a criticism, then there is no way for you to grow as a person and be better at life. You will live in a bubble where no one can say anything to you at all and everything will suffer for it.

Person Eating: "Hey, the dishes taste a little like dish soap. Can you give them an extra rinse?"
Dishwasher: "I don't taste the soap."
Person Eating: "You smoke, it's possible that you can't taste it but the rest of us do."
Dishwasher: "So I guess I do everything wrong then. Jesus Fucking Christ."
(#true story#)

Can you see how ridiculous this leap is? If there is soap residue on the dishes and everyone can taste it but you, then just rinse the dishes a little bit more before setting them to dry. It's the courteous thing to do. This is not an attack on your person, it's not a character assassination, however, if you don't taste the soap but everyone around you does, that doesn't mean the soap isn't there just because you don't taste it, and it is also not belittling.

This is belittling:
"Hey, the dishes taste like soap. Give them an extra rinse or are you too stupid to figure that out? You must be a total fucking waste of human flesh to, one, not be able to taste it, then two, not know how to rinse a fucking dish. For fuck's sake, who the fuck taught you how to wash dishes anyway, a fucking moron?" That is probably what you hear if you take everything personally. You hear an attack. You hear the assassination of your fragile ego. You, for some reason, think that if someone doesn't like the way you've done something, then there is nothing about you that is good or worthy of love. That, my fucked-up friends, is total bullshit and I'm gonna call out your Trolls. (see Step 7) You've got a serious fucking Troll problem.

From my own personal experience, criticism came easy from those around me, most notably my parents but since we are adults and we are no longer allowed to blame our parents for anything, I had to find a way to get rid of this tendency. Art school helped. I went to a photography school right out of high school. Maybe that was a bad idea. It was really fucking expensive and I didn't have any money for that. This was in the days before digital, it was all film. You couldn't buy an SD card for $20 and get 10,000+ shots. You bought rolls of film, $3 or $5 or more depending on the format; if it was 35mm, you had upwards of 36 shots to get it right and you wouldn't know until you processed the film, which could be *hours later.* Now you snap the shutter and you instantly know if you have the shot. So, photography school. I wasn't the best, but I wanted to be like Annie. Annie Leibovitz was/is my photography idol. Her work is breathtaking. I always turned my camera to people and while at The Ohio Institute of Photography, which is gone forever, I studied portraiture.

I was given a lot of criticism about my work, some of it hurt, especially when I thought what I had created was pretty cool but it made me a better photographer. Art is subjective, right? Just because you don't like it doesn't mean it's not good. Or, maybe it's not good but someone else can still like it. My mother has a piece of mixed media art that I just *don't* get. She thinks its the bee's knees and delights in it, which is wonderful. Art is supposed to move you in some way and it moves her to joy. I look at that and I think, "If I owned that, I'd give it to the thrift store." I've told her as such about that piece of art when she asked me what I thought about it but not about the thrift store. That would have been mean. I said, "I don't think I like this one as much as other pieces in your collection." She has others that I think are amazing but that one does nothing for me. The issue is that she takes it personally that I don't like *that* particular piece. My not liking that piece of mixed media art has nothing to do with her self-worth or her choices, her preferences; it has *nothing* to do with her. Again, she has three other pieces in her house that if I could hide them in my bag and scurry them out of there without her knowing, they'd be mine. She could ask me what about it doesn't speak to me, she could ask me what about her other curated pieces do; but instead she gets a bit upset that I don't like that *one* thing. Even if I say that I adore Umbrella Man on Red by Peter Max, which she has hanging in her foyer, or the piece by I-don't-know-who that she has hanging over the mantle, she will get hung up on the one that I don't like. You gotta let that shit go. Just fuckin' let it ride, people.

I had a piece that I did in photography school of a guy I knew. He played guitar. I shot on infrared film, which isn't normally used for portraiture, and the resultant images were rather cool. I printed one up, matted it and submitted for the school photography show. Snagged a second-place ribbon. I showed it to the owner of the portrait studio where I worked and all he did was compare it to the cookie cutter portraits that they were known for; it didn't fit in his mind of what a portrait was and therefore, to him, it was no good. It was good enough to the judges to get a ribbon so I shrugged it off. I was happy with it and the subject of the portrait was happy with the results. Fuck all to everyone else.

How about this: are you the kind of person who thinks that every idea is a bad idea because you didn't think of it? Is it hard for you to consider that maybe someone has a better idea about something that you care about? Is it difficult for you to consider that you might not know everything about something that you love? Do you get pissed off when someone is better at something than you are even if it is something that you don't care about? Do you tend to not ever want anyone's help on anything ever because you don't want to feel stupid? Is it possible that you don't know everything? Is it possible that someone accidentally demonstrating to you that you don't know everything is the worst possible thing that could happen to you?

It is okay to not be good at something.
It is okay to not know everything about a subject that you love.
It is okay to not be the smartest person in the room when it comes to any one thing.
It is okay to learn from those around you, even children.
It is okay to be fallible and in the process of learning.
It is okay.

◆ ◆ ◆

Anecdote Time!
I worked in an office after doing construction for about four years. I was tired of being dirty all the time and ended up getting an office job. I remember the first week at the new office: I felt like a rat trapped in a cage. Despite being tired of being dirty while doing construction, sitting in an office at a cubicle felt like I was trapped. The other reason why I don't like to work in corporate office environments is because of the politics and the stupid games that get played. For example, when I was working at this place, I was reasonably slender. [Now that I've had two kids, my body has changed but I'm working on that. My health depends on it.] There were several women in this office, on my floor, that had been working there for a lot longer than me. When I started, I was polite and kind to everyone and I made sure to listen to those around me because they had been there longer, knew the work and I had a lot to learn anyway. There was one woman who was rather cold to me and when I asked for help or had questions, her answers were always rather short and dismissive. Okay, whatever. After a few weeks, she warmed up a bit as I continued to be polite and nice despite her chilly attitude towards me. One day, I came in, saw her and gave a friendly "Good morning!" and she just stared at me as I walked by with a maybe-less-than-neutral look on her face and she certainly didn't respond with a 'good morning' of her own. I thought to myself, "I wonder who pissed in her Post Toasties today?" and I let it go. Her bad attitude was not my problem; I didn't cause it directly since I just got there. A little bit later, after continued nasty looks and completely ignoring me when I was asking questions, I went to the supervisor to ask my question. I said, "Hey, what's going on with What's-Her-Name? She's been rather abrupt with me today." The supervisor said, "Oh, she decided last night before we went home that she doesn't like you anymore." <*insert record scratch*> Um, okay. That's pretty much what the supervisor said to me, I don't think I'll ever forget that because it was such a poignant moment for me. I hadn't done anything to this person besides exist in the same general area as her. I was never mean, I didn't talk about her behind her back other than to ask the supervisor if there was a problem I had inadvertently caused, this decision of What's-Her-Name's was completely on her own. I could have taken it personally. I could have been really upset that, where before there was a least a somewhat cordial work environment, had now turned hostile towards me. I did nothing directly to cause this, it was something this other person decided in their mind. I said to the supervisor, "Oh, okay. Then it was nothing I did" and I went on about my day.

The point of all that was I hadn't made a mistake that reflected badly on What's-Her-Name. I hadn't insulted her. I hadn't done anything directly to her in any way for her to have a negative perception of me. She decided in her mind, for whatever reason, that I was no longer to be liked. Fine. That's her choice. Whatever. I stopped asking her for help. I didn't avoid her but I didn't engage. To me, she became furniture unless I had to interact with her directly. There was no point subjecting myself to her vitriol and negativity, so I steered around. What her choice didn't do was affect how I saw *myself*. I didn't take her desire to not be cordial to me as a personal attack. If she doesn't like me for whatever reasons she's drummed up, that's cool, but it has absolutely nothing to do with *me*. I didn't return the behavior, though. I remained neutral to her. I didn't see the point in making the experience of working in an office even worse by stirring up shit.

If you didn't do anything and someone has decided that they don't like you, that's their thing. Not yours. If you did do something and it was an honest mistake, then fess up and fix it. If you did do something and it wasn't an honest mistake and you are trying to create drama, well, that makes you an asshole.

Stop it.

Let's talk about Always and Never and maybe a little bit of "I told you so." I'm not a huge fan of any of these. Let's start with Always and Never. These two fucking punks. I really just don't like these words and the reason is because the live in the realm of absolutes, there is no gray area with these two fuckers.

Always: this little fucking adverb states that it is "at all times; on all occasions" according to the dictionary. This doesn't allow for any wiggle room and I'm a huge fan of wiggle room. Here's how Always gets along so well with taking everything so fucking personally.

Someone says, "You are always angry." This explicitly states that you exist in no other state than angry. At all times and on all occasions, you are angry. There is no other state of being. Let's say that you got angry over something small, the straw that broke the camel's back as we say, and there was a burst of general anger at an overall shitty day. This anger was brief and directed at no one, merely a pop of the stress valve to let off a burst of steam, because you broke a nail after getting a manicure or you realized that you forgot one small thing at the hardware store after having gone there seven times before to pick up other things you'd already forgotten. Little nuisances that build up over time into a giant Shit Sundae and someone happens to be nearby when The Cherry of Aggravation gets put on top. If that someone who was nearby happens to be the someone who takes everything personally, they will not be able to discern that they had nothing to do with your anger over the forgotten tool or the broken nail, they will be unable to figure out or understand that there was a whole day (or days) of bullshit stacked up behind that one final thing that sent the Sisyphean ball back down the fucking hill. They are unable to realize that they had nothing to do with any of it at all. All they see is the outburst, even if it is relatively mild, and they take it personally. That moment is the "always" moment: you are always angry and they will remember this forever. Unless that person goes through the personal change of understanding and learning how not to take things personally then it will be a no-win situation. Even if you are very clear and say, "This has nothing to do with anyone, I've just had a shitastic week" they will still feel like you are yelling *at* them, that you are mad *at* them, they will *not* hear/care/understand that you are not because this is what they do.

This was said to me once. It irked me. I am not always angry. I think that would be a very difficult state to maintain. Then, time passed and I was having a great time, laughing, carrying on, being silly and I said to this person, "Am I angry right now?" They said, "...no..." and I responded, "then I *am not* always angry" and walked away. I'm not a fan of "I told you so" but this is my way of saying it without saying it.

I've learned this lesson. This one is difficult and it sucks balls. Now, when people get angry around me, I feel uncomfortable. I think most people do or would. I don't immediately feel that I am to blame for their anger, though, and I allow the anger to happen as I think that all emotions are okay as long as they are not violent and are based in some sort of reality. If I know for a fact that I did nothing to stoke this anger, then I needn't take anything personally.

Never is exactly the same but in reverse. Another adverb, this one is "at no time, on no occasion" so it, too, lives in the realm of absolutes. We could just switch the above-mentioned scenario around and have it be a Never instead of an Always. "You are never happy." That implies that at no point is there joy, about anything. This, much like anger, is a very difficult state to maintain. Some people who take things too personally cannot seem to really process much other than joy or happiness; *that* they understand. If others are feeling joy and happiness, then whatever that person is feeling is easier to handle because it's going to take the edge off their own feelings, which they might have a hard time rectifying. If someone has a very hard time handling or processing emotions and making heads or tails of them, (anything other than joy or happiness, which are big and obvious) they're going to be difficult to be around.

Let's say someone has a resting bitch face but that person is feeling rather neutral at that moment. Maybe they are concentrating on something or just thinking and in their own world. Someone who takes everything so personally might think that the person is mad when they are not. Without specifically asking if that person is angry, then we would not know what they are feeling as their state is neutral. Many of us tend to default back to neutral or slightly to one side of neutral, either a tad bit happy or a tad bit unhappy, on any old regular day but throughout the day, these emotions will vacillate slightly. However, someone who takes everything so personally will not have the desire or the ability to ask those questions. They will just make an assumption and the assumption will be to the negative side: You are never happy, you are always angry therefore your neutral state is always going to be negative especially if you've expressed a negative emotion in the past. They remember the bad and not the good. This puts the other person at a disadvantage all the time. They will have to fight to prove that they are not feeling whatever the person who takes everything so personally thinks. The relationship might consistently feel like an uphill battle. Fuck that shit.

If you do have a bad day and express an emotion that is not obvious joy or happiness, then their hypothesis of "You are always angry/you are never happy" will be proved. They will point at you and say "A-HA! I knew it! See? You ARE angry right now, you are not happy, therefore I was right!" and that's where it will stay because once that emotion has faded and the situation is back to whatever normal is, they will still be sitting in their little baby pool of perceived victory with a big ass banner that says "I told you so." I don't like to revel in moments like I described above where, while happy, I asked the other person if I was still always angry; I try not to say "I told you so" because I hope that these situations present themselves to the other person to show them the error of their ways. Sometimes the other person does not see this so I might gently point it out. I fucking hate hypocrisy, even in myself. However, the risk is run of the other person, the one who takes things way too fucking personally, feeling persecuted or harassed and around and around we go again. Fucking exhausting.

I don't think anyone actually enjoys being told they are wrong or being proved wrong. That feels really fucking icky, however we grow as people when we are able to see that there was wrongness and then go about fixing it. What is better for everyone is if those around the person who is fixing the wrongness can see and acknowledge that the fixing is taking place and then let that shit go. I felt for a long time that some people in my family had this construct of me that was way outdated. They still thought that I was the same person at 32 that I was at 15. That is grossly unfair. As people grow and change, we have to adjust our view of them to accept this new information. If the person is not growing and changing, and if we care about them, we should try to find ways to bring them current, so to speak, so that they are growing, evolving and adapting as a person to the world that is constantly changing around them.

If, after reading this, you have the ability to see that maybe you are a person who takes things way too personally, then I encourage you to seek out a counselor who will remain neutral and will help you drill down to exactly why you feel this way. This counselor needs to be someone you feel completely at ease with but you also absolutely need to open your fucking mouth and talk. Not about the weather or your frustrations with your boss at work. You need to talk about the hard shit. You have to get past the superfluous and get to the meat. Fucking open your damn mouth and *talk.*

There was a counselor I saw who used the example I gave earlier about the portrait I did of the guy with the guitar as a metaphor for me. My boss at the portrait studio didn't like the piece. It didn't fit in with his idea of what a good portrait was. This didn't make the piece not good because others thought it was good enough to earn a second-place ribbon in a photo show. My opinion of the picture was that the guy in it was delighted with the image, that made me happy as the artist; I was happy with the ribbon it earned and so, to me, the picture was good. My boss' opinion didn't matter, just like What's-Her-Name deciding not to like me anymore. That didn't diminish me as person in the slightest. I had nothing to do with the formation of her opinion, she just changed her mind based on some internal reference point and that was that. I still moved about my day and life as if nothing changed because nothing had. If What's-Her-Name got mad near me for some reason, I was not in a position to automatically assume that it was me she was mad at or the reason for her anger. If I knew that I was in no way responsible for it, why should I internalize that and take it personally? I shouldn't and I don't. That's why I asked if I accidentally did something that upset her. If I had, I would have tried to fix it. I'm not the kind of person who goes about purposefully pissing people off. That is usually not my intention. I don't have the time or the energy for vindictiveness and neither should you. If you are vindictive, please try to find a way to use your powers for good and not evil. Don't be an asshole.

Being able to discern when someone is really trying to hurt you by saying horrible things to bring you down specifically or if they are just being a dick and having a moment is pretty key to being able to move forward in life. If you approach life with a fucking battle mentality, that every damned day is going to be a fucking uphill battle of defeating your enemies at every turn... oh man, that's just exhausting. I don't think many of us have that many nemeses. Not everyone is out to get you or bring you down, that's just not the way these things work. Looking for enemies at every turn requires a lot of fucking energy that is better spent on other things, people.

In *Step 8: Obsess Much?* I mention my shitty neighbor, Harvey. He seems to spend a lot of time trying to come up with ways to make my life miserable. I don't know him that well because there is no having a conversation with him. Before things got shitty, I had maybe two convos with the man. I realized pretty quickly that he seemed to be someone that takes things very personally, even things that only happen in his mind. Know what I mean? That's why I mention him more in Obsess Much? because sometimes we can create these fantastical scenarios in our heads, detailed and fucking nuanced, of shit that hasn't even happened yet and probably won't happen the way it is being dreamed up but then a whole emotional life and response is being crafted around this fucking fantasy. Before we know it, we are living emotionally in this fantasy that has absolutely fuck all to do with the real world. People are seeing responses to nothing and might say "what the fuck is *wrong* with you?" and they mean that. If you think you might be doing this, then find that counselor. Explain that there are these whole other fucking fantasy worlds of shit happening in your head that are not based on any sort of reality and instead are just crafted fantasies made solely to stoke your emotional life into a fucking shitstorm that is then projected on to everyone around you.

> "When you think everything is someone else's fault, you will suffer a lot. When you realize that everything springs only from yourself, you will learn both peace and joy." ~ His holiness the 14th Dalai Lama

SECTION 2: FANTASY THINKING

> "The problem with fantasy is the greatest benefit of fantasy: it prevents us from living in the present moment." ~Geneen Roth

Remember this: "Da plane! Da plane!" says Tattoo.

"Welcome to Fantasy Island!" That was always worth the wait. Watching Richard Montalbán say that line was the best. I remember squealing with glee because shit was about to get not-real for those people. Everyone said they loved it when Tattoo squawked from the tower and rang the bell but nah, for me it was the toast of champagne and the declaration of being in a fantasy.

Cue the cheesy 1970s violin music.

Man, I loved that show. I think it was on Friday nights right after Love Boat...or maybe Love Boat was on later and Fantasy Island was on first. I don't remember but I do remember sitting on the floor with a pillow and a blanket at my grandparent's house, right in front of their console TV, all snuggled up in their creepy ass house to watch this double feature. I remember how the fantasies that the guests had were usually fairly run-of-the mill, nothing too scandalous for the 70s but something would usually go horribly awry and it would turn out that the guest would think better of their fantasy. They'd walk away from their experience being not only $50,000 lighter (in 1970s money, which is about $315,000 now) but also more woke about what was going on in their lives and what they needed to fix. Or just realizing that they are stupid.

We all have fantasies. Some are pretty mundane. "I have a fantasy that I'll never have to wash another dish ever again." And some are pretty saucy...

That's fine. Sauce it up a bit, get after it and daydream about that cute guy or girl ... but fantasies aren't always fun and exciting. Sometimes we get lost in fantasy thinking that is downright destructive; thinking that is hurtful to ourselves and not based on any kind of legit reality.

Daydreaming is healthy and it can be fun but what is not healthy or fun is thinking that your fantasies are real. Having the ability to discern what is real from what is fantasy is critical. Again, critical thinking: get some. Our mind is such a fertile fucking garden. Any number of beautiful things can be planted in it and tended to the point of harvest. (Am I losing you with the fucking analogy?) Sadly, many gardens are overrun with weeds. Or in my case, Trolls. Not those pesky, yet kinda cute, garden gnomes from the Harry Potter world, specifically in the Weasley's garden. I'm talking about big ass, dirty little fucking asshole twatball Trolls.

Also, you might want to put your finger on this page and jump quickly to Section 3, step 9, and read about Now and Later, then come back here.

STEP 5: STOP WISHING AWAY YOUR LIFE

> "People don't want to hear the truth because they don't want their illusions destroyed." ~Friedrich Nietzsche

My dad used to say something to me when I said the words "I wish..." followed by whatever. He would say "Shit in one hand and wish in the other and see which one fills up faster." Or he'd say something about a wish sandwich, you know, where you have two pieces of bread and wish you had some meat... Then he'd go off in a peal of laughter and say "Rrrrrrrubber biscuit!" My dad could be fucking hilarious. That is probably where I get my sense of humor, from my dad. He was never politically correct but he was really fucking funny.

Wishing upon a star. Wishing on a dandelion puff. Wishing on ripping the petals off some poor unsuspecting flower. Birthday candles, eyelashes, wishbones, fuckin' ladybugs, lottery tickets and leprechauns, white animals and fountains. Hey, instead of throwing your coins in the water feature, just throw them to me and I'll see about getting that wish granted. The odds are about the same.

First off, I enjoy playing the lottery. Here's the part I like: the anticipation of it all; the not knowing. A bit of Schrödinger's cat but with a lottery ticket. Remember Schrödinger's cat from the start of the book? Here is a bit from Wikipedia as a reminder.

> **Schrödinger's cat:** a cat, a flask of poison, and a radioactive source are placed in a sealed box. If an internal monitor (e.g. Geiger counter) detects radioactivity (i.e. a single atom decaying), the flask is shattered, releasing the poison, which kills the cat. The Copenhagen interpretation of quantum mechanics implies that after a while, the cat is simultaneously alive and dead. Yet, when one looks in the box, one sees the cat either alive or dead not both alive and dead. This poses the question of when exactly quantum superposition ends and reality collapses into one possibility or the other.

This cat exists in two states at once and in one iteration of the experiment, the cat stays that way until it is observed and the act of observing the cat, such as peeking into the box to check on the kitty, could actually be what causes its demise.

The movie The Matrix: love it or hate it, I don't care. (Just channeled The Michael Stanley Band there for a second.) Neo goes to see The Oracle. He bumps the vase, it breaks. She says that she'll get one of the kids to fix it later, then says "What's really going to bake your noodle later on is, would you still have broken it if I hadn't said anything?" That sort of thing. The lottery ticket for me is $2 worth of being and thinking "What would I do with [so many] millions of dollars when I win?" and between the time I buy the ticket and the numbers are drawn, I allow myself this little fantasy. Then I hear that someone won, I don't want to hear in what city or state because for just a moment, it is me. I then think about the flood of emotions I will feel when I realize that all of my numbers match and I play out this little drama in my head. How I would break the news to my husband, what I would do first, who would I tell, and so on. It is a fun little program that runs in the back of my head, sort of on autoplay.

Here's what I don't do between the time I've purchased the lottery ticket and the drawing of the numbers: *nothing.*

The lottery isn't a retirement plan. It is not my plan for anything. It is a wish, it is a fucking fantasy. It is not real (until it is) and it cannot be relied on. I honestly think that winning the lottery could be the worst fucking thing that could ever happen to me. Watch, it'll probably happen now because I said that...though the odds are astronomical. We say "astronomical" but still, even with the Fermi Paradox, the Drake equation hints that it is still a possibility, just like winning the lottery. That is, unless you think Frank Drake is full of shit, which is entirely possible, too. He is and he isn't until we find that planet that has life on it outside our solar system.

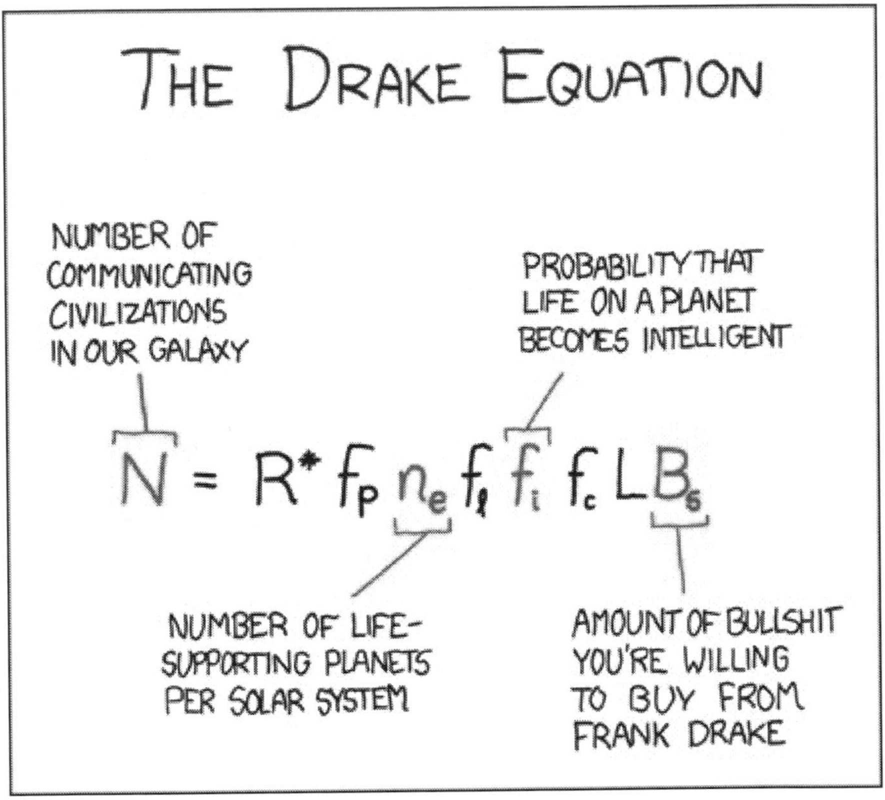

I stole this from xkcd.com and I love it so much.

What's my point of this fucking tangent? Wish. Daydream. Have a little afternoon fantasy. However, you need to come back from that shit, like leaving a movie theater, and walk out in to the glaring brightness of the day and realize that it was all just a fucking fantasy. Your real life is out here, with us. Take the fucking red pill, people. Reality is what you want and need. Your fantasy life is a great place to hang out when you need a mental break. We all do it and for some, it is absolutely necessary but we all need to come back and do our work.

Here's the thing about my lottery fantasy. When I think about all that money, I wonder what I would spend it on. I know that I would eliminate all my bills first, which is mostly just student loans and my mortgage at this point. I would buy a car that is more reliable than my 18-year-old Nissan that I love dearly but really is showing its age, but not flashy because then I would have to spend a shit ton of money just to insure and maintain that. I'd probably hook up the hubs with a newer truck for his work. We both agree that neither of us would entirely give up work. It's too fulfilling and we are both self-employed. Of course, we say this now without the money and maybe having more money than you could possibly spend would change that perspective. I don't think I could spend $559 million dollars, or whatever the take home of that is, in one life. I also don't think I would want to. I'm not into hookers and blow, so...

My lottery fantasy gets me to focusing on what I would spend the money on and then that gets me thinking about what I really want money for in the first place. This allows me to focus on my work and its purpose: why am I doing what I do. After all of this, I have a bit of razor focus on what is important in my life and how I delegate my money. I know that I would probably stay anonymous, as much as possible, and keep my kids doing what they are doing. That is, until the anonymity is ruined, then we'd have to run for the hills. Having built two businesses in our town, I say that I don't think I would want to abandon those but again, I can't say as I haven't won the lottery to be able to tell specifically what I would do.

This is all fantasy. All of it. Until it actually happens, it is not real. I cannot base my life or my decisions on that specific thing. Okay, so you know how they say to flip a coin if you can't make a decision and whichever thing you are thinking/hoping for while the coin is in mid-air is your true heart's desire? Yeah, I use the lottery fantasy to boil down my most important financial goals. Pay off my shit, yo. No debt. A decent car, maybe brand new. Maybe not. My son says, "Would you buy a sports car?" and I give him some side eye and say, "No. I would not. No good place for a car seat and I'd get pissed that you got food smooshed in the seats. I'd be too worked up over it so no... but I might buy a sweet ass Cadillac. Like a CTS or CTS-V." He nods his head, knowingly, but it would have a strict "no eating or drinking in the car" policy.

If I want a Cadillac, and probably not a CTS, anytime soon, then I need to hunker down and leave my fantasy life where it is and get some fucking work done. Every morning, I am up around 4am to sit at my desk and write. I write every day. Sometimes I don't write books, sometimes I just write letters and send those to people. I have to write papers for school. I have to have cogent thoughts and be able to put those in writing. I can get up and fucking troll Facebook for three hours, hop on Pinterest and daydream about all those fun looking crafty things and waste all my fucking productive time or I can get up and do the fucking work.

Do the fucking work.

Flip your eggs.

Level up.

Let's talk about Facebook and Pinterest and how they are fantasy. This has been well documented and there is a plethora of studies done on how they fuck up your perception of the world and how you see yourself in that world so fuck that shit. It is just like I tell my kids: if it is on a screen and/or from the Internet, there's a good chance that it is probably fantasy. This gets them, mostly my son as my daughter just says "I want my show" and plops her diapered bum in her spot on the couch to watch Thomas and Friends on an endless fucking loop, if she had her druthers, to think critically about what he is seeing both online and onscreen when we are watching the television. He asks about the news, "Is this real or fantasy?" and I say, "Sometimes it is hard to tell."

Critical thinking, people. Get some.

Tons of research exists about how people are not being truthful about themselves on social media. They stage Instagram photos to make it seem like more than it actually is. They'll only post photos from their trips and nothing about how they ended up pants-less in a ditch, without any money and confused after getting jumped in some tourist town. I don't know. I'm making shit up. My point is that people only seem to put their best foot forward on social media and that foot has been seemingly professionally styled. It is a fantasy of the reality of that person and in no way should be construed as the truth. Being able to discern fantasy from reality is really kinda fucking key, people. Don't be a gullible moron. Question it all. All of it. Ask questions, dig deep, demand answers! (Oh. Uh, an exclamation point. I rarely use those. I must mean it.) Research The Shed at Dulwich. Go. I'll wait.

Let's just put it this way, the less time you spend swiping about on social media platforms and seeing what everyone else is doing and having stupid acronym feelings, FOMO, (gah, so stupid; the acronym, not the feeling, that is real), you will get nothing done in your real offline life. I'm not talking about people who make their living managing social media accounts for businesses or personalities. I get that there are legit reasons to be on that stuff more than normal. That's fine but you still have to put that shit down. Just put it the fuck down and walk away from it. Eyes up here, people. Up here. Yes. Where the real world is. Yes, I know that the real world can totally suck balls most of the time but we need y'all to be present in this one to make it better.

I love the Internet, I do. I think it's fucking fantastic. But I also like reality. I like being present in my moments as much as I can be and this is a huge reason why I don't drink or take drugs. In order for me to be present in my moments, I have to be unaltered. I'd like you to consider an unaltered life, too, specifically from the fantasy of social media. In my opinion, social media is just another way to wish away your life.

Stop it.

I like social media. I have social media accounts. I do not *live* on social media and you shouldn't either. (Disclaimer: my exception to this is as such: there are people out there making a living as "Influencers", which is a new word in English. I get that. I understand it. It's not my bag. All I ask is that whatever you are influencing is helping make the real world a better place.)

STEP 6: THE GRASS AIN'T ANY FUCKING GREENER OVER THERE

> "If the grass is greener on the other side it's probably getting better care. Success is a matter of sticking to a set of common sense principles anyone can master." ~ Earl Nightingale

"Things will get better when..."

Shut the fuck up.

"If I just get that job, then..."

Really? Shut the fuck up. Again.

"Maybe if I uproot my whole life and move to..."

Shit ain't gonna be any better when you get there.

Wanna know why?

Because your shit follows you.

It's the worst fucking stalker ever. Except maybe the ones that kill you. Those are the worst.

I suffered from this, the Grass Is Greener Syndrome. If you are unfamiliar with this, let me drop some knowledge. It is basically the feeling that things will be better if only a certain thing would happen, or maybe a skill is acquired, or you learn something new. It is a little like a horse with a carrot. That carrot is always out front, just out of reach and the horse keeps going for it but never quite gets it and is never satisfied with what is in front of it, like the grass under his feet, which he could eat right now if he wanted to but instead is only focused on the thing he can't get, the carrot.

Constantly looking to the Later and Maybe If-fing yourself does no one any good. Make some plans, that's fine but have those plans be based on something other than a fantasy. Remember when I talked about the lottery ticket and what I was actually buying with those two dollars? I was buying the fantasy, the daydream and the anticipation. There are so many people who live in this place. This place of constant soon-ness. Don't get me wrong, I like looking forward to things. My new sister-in-law is putting together a surprise party for my brother and I am looking forward to that. That should be a scream. I could look forward to the day when I am not trying to decide between buying gas or buying groceries because I don't have enough money for both. I can sit in any one of these daydreams and do nothing, or I could do something, anything, that will get me closer to my goals.

It's Sunday. Do you really think I like getting up at 3:30am to work? No, I don't, but here I am with a cup of coffee, a cat to the right of me, and I'm working on something. You know what I haven't done since I started writing this manuscript?

Bought a lottery ticket.

I don't need the fantasy right now of winning the lottery because I am making forward progress with something that is real and tangible. If you think that I don't have moments where I'm scared shitless, you'd be completely and utterly wrong. I never look like it but I'm scared half the time. Scared of making the wrong decision *again*, scared of speaking my mind, scared of having an opinion, scared of not being smart enough, scared of what someone might think. Most of the time, I tell myself that I cannot care about these things, that I have to push forward and that I really have no choice. I've been homeless, I've been destitute and I got through all that shit. I can get through someone's opinion.

I cannot live in the fantasy of the places with green grass when the grass I have right here is just fine.

I'm actually no fan of real grass. That is a conversation for another day but that shit requires a ton of fucking maintenance. I think I read somewhere (unverified, I might add) that lawn mowers contribute a disgusting amount of pollution to the environment including noise pollution. Fuck that shit. I'd very much like to rip up most of my lawn and put in something less demanding. Fuck you, Grass, with your fertilizers and your constant mowing and your fucking grubs. Fuck you.

Remember when we talked about the Now and that Now was really all you had. With the Grass Is Greener Syndrome you are fucking squandering that precious Now with the Later, shit that hasn't happened, probably won't happen and if it does, you won't be happy with it anyway. I fucking moved from Ohio to Los Angeles on a fucking whim. Uprooted everything. I gave up my sweet ass place to live, I gave up friends and social connections I had made, my job was online so that came with me, but I just packed up my shit, my dog and my cat (both dead now <*sad face*>) and I moved to LA because I thought that when I got there, everything was going to be better or easier.

I couldn't have been more wrong. I got there and life got worse. So much worse. The twatwaddle I'd moved with now had me separated from friends and family, isolated 2,500 miles away from my network and he began his mental and emotional abuse of me. I had culture shock. I had the stress of moving my 2,100 sq foot stuff into a 650 sq foot apartment, that included his stuff, too. I had to deal with being stranded. While I was working, he would take my car and just be gone for hours, leaving me stuck in the apartment needing to figure out the bus route. But fuck that shit. That was **my** car, you ride the fucking bus, you fucking twat.

Anyway, I digress.

I thought life would get better and eventually it did but at first it got worse. For about 7 months, it was hellish for me. He was fucking horrible. I was isolated in every way. I had to fight to get out. I had to fight at every turn for things that felt normal and sane. He once tried to get me to admit that I had OCD because I cleaned the kitchen. I had to make new friends and do you know how hard that is to do when you're an adult? I can attest to the fact that the friends I did make, I have kept even after being back in Ohio for all these years. The grass did not get greener. Have you been to LA? The grass is either really rough and not fun to walk on or its dead and burnt from the sun, or wildfires.

After the twat went to Panama to work on an America Ferrera movie, I made my move...to Studio City. This was after he destroyed my car in a wreck, not his fault; it was the other driver's fault but I feel better when I blame him for that. (I know. I know. Go back to Step 2, EB.) I was 6 months away from paying it off and I'm the kind of person who keeps a car until it falls apart all Blues Brothers style. I was driving this 1987 Ford EXP with no air conditioning and an incredibly small trunk. I rented a tiny guest house that ended up being infested with termites. I went from 2,100 sq ft in Ohio to 650 sq ft in downtown LA to just over 300 sq ft in Studio City. Granted, the house in Studio City had a pool and tons of outdoor living space, but still. Tiny and infested with bugs. Good times. I did meet some awesome people, the guys who rented the front house, Matt, Nate and Mason. Things got better and LA is where my personal growth path truly started.

I remember laying by the pool on a cool December day. Not quite warm enough to make me want to get in the pool but cool enough to lay in the sun with the dog. She was curled up with me and we were dozing. I remember thinking that not much, really, had gotten better. That despite my zip code changing, I still had the same problems in LA that I had in Columbus. Nothing changed. And in hindsight, what seems so obvious now hit me like a ton of bricks. I remember the feeling and the scene so clearly. I'm lying on the concrete, no lounge chair, no blanket. Just lying on the concrete pool deck. Jenna is laying along my right side, she's dozing peacefully in the sun and I'm completely unaware that cancer is riddling her body and will soon take her from me as quickly as she entered my life.

I took this the night before she died. It was the last time she could sit up on her own.

We are quiet. We are peaceful. I'm letting my mind wander but not into sleep. I don't want to sleep. I just want to be in the Now. I wanted to take that minute and fucking appreciate where I was. I was laying by a pool, *my* pool in a way, sure it was kinda shitty and needed thousands of dollars of repair work but it was still my pool, I took care of it; with my beloved dog, in Los Fucking Angeles, California, a city that held such fascination and awe for me as a child when I first visited with my dad. I thought that California was magic and I still do. When you come from Ohio, The Golden Coast of California is fucking magic. My hand is draped over the belly of my dog, the sun is dappled through the leaves of the locust tree that shaded part of the yard and dropped innumerable leaves into the pool. It was quiet, even for LA. Our part of Studio City was a quiet little residential area. Older families, older homes, tucked into the little nook made by the 101/170/134 freeways, (never had I lived anywhere where the freeways were referred to as "the 101". In Ohio, we just say, "Take 71 south". If I said, "Take *the* 71 South," people would think I was nuts but I never noticed that I started using the *the* when I moved there. I just did.) We were near Moorpark and Tujunga. I loved it there not because it was the best house or anything like that but it was freedom. I was free. And, while I was free, I let my mind go. I just laid there and I appreciated everything that got me to that moment. The Twat was gone, my dog was there, I made new friends, I was pursuing something that I really loved to do and I felt good, but when I thought about all the shit and why things were still going the way they had always gone, I had that 'ton-of-bricks' moment, an epiphany if you will; just like the one I had had a few decades ago in the kitchen of my house as a teenager: ***I*** was the common denominator for every shitty thing that ever happened to me. It was me all along. Like the big reveal in any suspenseful movie. It was *me* all along.

Moving to Los Angeles was one of the best things I've ever done despite all the pain and heartache that went with that. The gains and losses are not lost on me but it was there, by that pool, next to my shitty little house, with my beloved dog, that I realized that I had no one to blame but myself. For everything. In that moment, I stopped blaming my parents, I stop blaming others, and I only blamed myself. I had to take responsibility for all of it.

I cried. I didn't sob. I just quietly cried. Jenna heard me and moved so she could snarfle my face. She didn't like it when I cried and she would graciously let me sob into the fur of her neck when I needed to but this time, I didn't. I just needed her to know that I knew. I fucking knew that my shit was my own shit and I had to own that shit. I will not go far as to say that I had some sort of major personality overhaul. Nah. I still fuck up pretty regularly and I still own up to it. I am always striving to be better than I was the day before, to be clearer with my intentions, to have focus and clarity. That shit is pretty fucking hard and I am always impressed by and in awe of those who seem to have it. Laser focused, pin-point clarity. I gotta get me some of that. They don't deviate. They say no. They don't feel any remorse for doing that either. They don't play the victim and they take responsibility for their fuck ups and their failures but instead of letting those things drag them down to The

Edge of The Abyss, they use them as fuel to be better, do better. Let's be that, shall we?

♦ ♦ ♦

You know that platitude: Bloom where you are planted. Do you know that one? It shows up in memes and on coffee mugs and shit like that. I didn't like that saying at all. I was a tumbleweed, a dandelion seed, a wish in the wind. I did not have the ability to put down any kind of roots and lead a fucking stable ass life. I was constantly moving from apartment to apartment because I always thought that there was something better. In this quest for 'better', I ended up with a lot of shit because despite having a really hard time making a decision, I was constantly distracted by 'shiny things' (still am) and dashing from this to that and back to this again. It's all very exhausting but I was young and had the energy.

I remember when all the constant moving started to cause trouble. Friends didn't want to help me move anymore. My mail couldn't keep up with me and most importantly, but I wouldn't care about this until much later, my credit score started to suffer.

Ah, yes. The thing by which we all should measure our self-worth: Our credit score.

Seriously, though. I was constantly moving from apartment to apartment, guy to guy, job to job. Nothing was stable, nothing was secure, nothing was comfortable. I was always unsettled, always disrupted and then always complaining about all of those things. The banks wanted to know why I couldn't just sit in one spot for a while and be okay with that. I didn't really have any answer other than to say "But....over there..... Is....." And they'd just kind of glaze over in the eyes. Like I said, it was exhausting for everyone. I ended up squandering some really precious time. Time I could have spent building *something*.

STEP 7: KILL THE TROLLS IN YOUR HEAD

> "I have no pithy quote here. Sorry." ~ E.B. Davis II

You know what I'm talking about. There's a little fucker in your head right now. He sits there, along with all his shitty friends, all self-important, telling you all kinds of fucked up shit that you believe. Shit like you are not good enough, pretty enough or handsome enough, your abs aren't flat anymore and you *suck* because of it and so that makes you a piece of shit; you got a B so that means you're a stupid mother fucker, you didn't meet your quota so you are definitely going to get fired and...

Those are fucking Trolls and they need to die.

I'm not usually an advocate of violence but you need to fucking kill them.

Kill them dead!

Kill them now!!!!

Die!
Die!
Die!

Okay, deep breath.

Moving on.

My mother used to say to me when I'd fuck up a test in school, have a shitty day with a friend, or otherwise suck at life somehow, she'd say "Think of it as a learning experience" and I'd honestly hate to hear that. It wasn't very comforting and didn't help me much in the moment but it is surprisingly true, after the fact. If you make a mistake, a blunder, put your foot in your mouth, lose money, lose friends, whatever...You have to think of these things not as character flaws, unless you are Bernie Madoff and the like, but someone who needs to learn. The real problem is when you are stuck in a shitpile of Trolls who start berating you for your fuck up.

♦ ♦ ♦

Anecdote time!
My son brought home from school on Friday a small bottle of water with green coloring in it. The minute I saw this, I knew it was trouble. The bottle was from his lunch and he and his friend, who shall remain nameless, used markers to color the water green. He'd asked me for food coloring so he could make it more green, because that's *clearly* what needed to happen. How could I say no? I got the green food coloring and I made the requisite demands for carefulness and the moment I think he's being douchy with it, it's gone. I didn't say that word to him but he got the idea. He'd gotten a food prep glove from the cafeteria as he was a lunch helper on Friday and put clear water in it. He wanted to freeze it outside. Trial and error ensued and eventually he got a frozen hand. The husband and I are watching TV, uninterrupted, which is rare, and I said, "It's awful quiet. Where are the kids?" He shrugs. I holler out for the boy and he responds that he's in the bathroom with the little one and they are melting the hand in the sink with hot water.

What could go wrong?

A lot.

A few minutes goes by and the screaming starts. My son is screaming at the top of his fucking lungs, "My life is HELL!" [Troll alert], the little one is crying and comes into the living room, arms up, "MoooOOOoommy!" I said, "Go to daddy" and go to my son's room. The door has been slammed so many times that the hinges do not stay securely screwed to the frame anymore. I once took the door off because of the slamming and put up a blue curtain. Watching him try to slam a curtain was some of the funniest shit I have ever seen in my life. Anyway, he's *screaming* that his life is hell. That's privilege talking if I've ever heard it. I said, "Your life is hell? Really?" and with the news of the Turpin family out of California, which my son knew about, I said, "Those kids who were chained up and starved, that's a living hell. You've just made a mess and been inconvenienced."

The bottle of green water spilled all over the bathroom.

According to the boy, the little one grabbed at it and it splashed in to the trash can, which is metal mesh with a liner, and it ended up all over the toilet, the floor, the sink and so on. Four ounces of water can spread quite a distance. It was a mess, sure, but I could see where the water spilled because it was green so in that respect it was helpful. Instead of grounding him to his room or anything like that, I told him to go into his sister's room and help clean up that huge diorama they made with her blocks, cars, plastic ninjas, the entire cast of My Little Pony (minus Twilight Sparkle, she's hard to find in stores), her Mardi Gras beads, baby dolls and stuffed buddies. He protested, of course. My husband went in there and made the children clean up the room since both of them had built the thing anyway. I cleaned up the bathroom. I chose my battle.

◆ ◆ ◆

The point of that: That my son's head is fucking infested with shitty Trolls. I don't know how they got there... Actually, I do. He was born with them. I think that some people are born with Trolls in their heads. I was and I also think that there are people born relatively Troll-free or have a better handle on eradicating Trolls efficiently. I'm constantly mitigating the damage done by these asshole Trolls. The minute he fucks something up, and he will, for cryin' out loud, he's an eight-year-old boy. That's almost literally the definition of fucking shit up.

Fucking shit up *(phrasal verb)*: basically, an eight-year old-boy
I have to walk him back from The Edge of his personal Ledge and help him kill the

Trolls along the way. He will stand in his room or hide in the closet and just verbally and mentally beat himself up over and over and over about what he did wrong and how stupid he is and all sorts of just really wild stuff. In a way, it is amazing to watch. I've never said any of these things to him. I've never called him stupid or belittled him or anything like that. I would never! Yet, there he is, crying over whatever misstep or mistake he's made and it's just fucking hard core self-abuse. It's the Trolls.

The fucking Trolls.

Stop that shit.

If you do that to yourself, you need to stop.

What I tell him is that we'd never say that stuff to someone else and so we shouldn't say it to ourselves either.

I think most of us have done that some point. Standing in the bathroom, looking in the mirror at ourselves and thinking of all the things we *should* have said, all the things we *should* have done in the moment and then berating ourselves for not having done that. There's a reason that the saying goes "Hindsight is 20/20." Well, of course it is. We see everything so clearly after the fact but this does not mean that you should let the fucking Trolls have their way with you either. It is also why Alex Trebek is so smart: he has all the answers right in front of him.

Here's another take on it. I'm not a fashionable dresser. I'm really with Gilda Radner when it comes to fashion. If you are not familiar with Gilda Radner, I strongly implore you to seek out her work. She was truly one of the funniest women to ever live and she sadly and tragically died at 42 from ovarian cancer. She was one of the original cast members of *Saturday Night Live*, of which I would occasionally be allowed to watch as a kid. I loved Gilda then and I still do. She was the shit.

Gilda Radner once said that she bases her fashion choices on what doesn't itch and I agree with that. I'm not into being super fashionable. It has never been something that was important to me. I can rock a pair of jeans and a tee, maybe some cute shoes and jacket and that's about it. I don't really wear heels, and I don't like to be uncomfortable just to be hip. No thanks. I was in a class last semester and one of my much younger classmates said something about my sweater. I don't remember the comment exactly but she giving me shit about the color. It was in the purple range and she was throwing some shade. I said "Are you dissin' my sweater?" and she said that yeah, she was. First of all, I don't see the need to do that. If you don't like someone's clothing, just whisper some snarky comment to your friend under your breath, then you both laugh and that's that. That's what people usually do, right? Well, that would make you an asshole. Just a quiet one. Her comment wasn't necessary but I didn't take it personally. The sweater may not have been a super hip Color of the Moment but it is fucking cashmere and I fucking love cashmere. (Sorry, goats.)

It wasn't until much later that I thought of a few really clever things that I could have said but of course didn't. Then I started to doubt the sweater. "Should I be wearing that? Is it dated? Do I look stupid in it? Do I look like I'm straight out of 1987 while wearing that shade of purple?" I'd like to add right here that Pantone's Color of the Year for 2018 is Ultra Violet, number 18-3838, which is very similar in shade to the "questionable" sweater.

These are the Trolls talking.

I really shouldn't fucking care what she thought of my sweater and I honestly don't but the Trolls care. They care quite a bit. They fucking *live* for that kind of shit. If you have Trolls in your head making you fucking second guess yourself at every turn, then you need to find some way to get rid of the little fuckers. They are horrible and insidious. They will undermine all sorts of things that you do.

Are you an artist or want to be or enjoying something else that is completely subjective? Have you made something, written something, painted, sculpted, drawn, built, crafted something that you liked and fancied, that made you stand back and feel good about yourself? Then some asshole twatball comes along and says something like, "Eh, my little cousin, he's in first grade...yeah, they did that technique in their art class and his came out better." Maybe your asshole twatball "friend's" little cousin is the next fucking Great Master of art but that was a shitty thing to say and now your Trolls have their reason to come out from whatever little hole they live in and start undermining your feeling good about yourself. Fuck the Trolls and fuck your asshole twatball friend and their little cousin, too.

Fuck 'em all.

Trolls are a big reason why people don't bother to try whatever it is in their hearts and souls that they want to try. Whether it is trying to flip an egg for the second time ("I CAN'T!" ...Trolls) or going back to school ("I'm too old and stupid" ... Trolls) or writing a book ("No one wants to hear what I have to say"...Trolls) or anything else. You shouldn't fucking care but it is really hard not care about all that, isn't it? You hear these things being played over and over in your head and you're not entirely sure where they came from. Maybe someone did call you stupid once and that stuck, or you think that since you got a C- on a writing assignment in high school that you won't ever be a good enough writer to do a book. It is all bullshit. You have to know and you have to believe that it is all bullshit.

Remember earlier when I said that all we have is the Now and how fucking important it is to be in the Now and not constantly thinking about the future, or the Later, that hasn't happened yet? You have to take that little bit of Now, it is not very much but it's all you have, and in that moment, you have to be aware that there are little fucking Trolls in your head tying to tear everything the fuck down. You have to know they are there and you have to lock those little fuckers up, or kill them, or throw them out or whatever. When those thoughts pop up that start with "...but I can't because...., that's a Troll. You can try just pushing it away but it'll just come back. You have to think about that thought and maybe later you can really drill down to where that particular Troll came from and stop it at its source, but you have to be aware that it is there and then mentally create some sort of image in your head of you poisoning the Troll, bludgeoning it, or dropping it off a building or whatever other really graphic imagery that suits you, then do that. In your head. In that moment. Protect your precious Nows from the dirty little fucking asshole twatball Trolls.

You might think that is all you have to do but that little fucker will come back however, just like your eyebrow hairs, if you pluck them enough, they won't. This is a constant battle in your head. I won't stand here and say, "Oh, it's easy!" because it ain't. It is not easy. Battling the inner Trolls is so much harder than battling the outer ones, the ones that show up online or in your life. The ones in your outer life, they can just be ignored. I mean, you don't *have* to stand there and listen to them. It is just not necessary and if you think it is, then go back to the start of this and re-read the part about moving away from those that hurt you. It is called self-preservation, bitches. Do it.

The inner Trolls, oh, those assholes follow you everywhere. They are insidious and capricious and they multiply and before you know it, you can be overrun with the little fuckers. There are some people who either just don't have a lot of naturally occurring Trolls or they are really good at getting rid of them. I know what you are thinking... I think it, too...that is, if you are a person with a lot of naturally occurring Trolls and seem to be inexperienced at eradicating them...

How can I *not* care?

The only way I can tell you how to not care is to practice not caring. I know, so fucking stupid. It is like that advice at the beginning, "just *be* happy." Right? It is fucked up in its simplicity but yet it feels like it is not a good enough answer.

Start small. Stop caring about something small and I don't mean your kids. Yes, I know they are small but that's not the kind of small I'm referring to. If you are someone who has to make their bed every day or the world is just fucked, then stop caring about that. Maybe that's a small thing to me but a big thing to you. If you don't like that suggestion, find something else that is smaller and stop caring about it.

Here's the next question I hear you asking: How do I *do* that?

You make a choice.

Yes, I know. It's fucking maddening but it really is that simple. Earlier, I told you to choose a death for your inner Trolls. You had to think that about for a tick, then make a choice. Maybe you would choose a different death for a Troll the next time but you made a choice and then you tossed your Troll into the lava pit, or whatever, and dusted off your hands and went about your fabulousness. Good. Do that for not caring.

"Oh, look. I have a sink full of dishes that should probably be handled before I do anything important." (procrastination, that's coming up next.)

<Thinking about the dishes.... Choosing not to care right now>

Eventually you should probably do the dishes but for the Now, you have to not care. If, while you are doing whatever you are doing to make your life more fucking fantastic, the Dish Trolls show up and start harassing you about how shitty of a housekeeper you are and that if someone were to come over (which as we all know no one really does anymore. Seriously. When was the last time you had company?) and sees a sink full of dishes, your guests would be so fucking mortified [*gasp* <pearl clutch>], and the Trolls start fucking with you... Into the lava pit, you fucking little Dish Troll. Away with you, be gone.

Easy peasy pumpkin squeezy. That's how this works.

The thoughts come in that are not so nice (Trolls) and you have to mentally toss them into the 55-gallon drum filled with lye or whatever demise you have chosen. They come in, "Oh, hello dirty little fucking asshole twatball Troll. *<tosses into the drum and watches it bubble and dissolve>* Goodbye, dirty little fucking asshole twatball troll."
"Off you go, then."

Then you get back to work on your fabulousness.

Done.

Then the little shit returns. "Oh, you again?" *<sigh...toss>* back to work. Keep doing this until it gets to the point where the dirty little fucking asshole twatball Troll doesn't even bother poking his head out of his nasty hole to see what you are up to. Keep in mind that you will probably, at some point, have to go and do the dishes, however, it is okay to let them sit while you work on those things that are maybe not so fun but critically important to you progressing in a forwardly fashion through your life.

Many would say that these Trolls I speak of are nothing more than a lack of confidence in yourself or lack of self-esteem. Probably. But I think it is easier to think of these things are something that is there, hidden, because they are being stomped on by dirty little fucking asshole twatball Trolls. If you weed the garden, so to speak, then the flowers can bloom. The Trolls are your weeds. So many analogies.

Maybe this part should be at the beginning but we're all adults here, I'm assuming, so I figured y'all would know the difference between self-confidence and self-esteem. This is an assumption I've made that should at least be mentioned. Self-confidence is how you feel about your abilities in any one thing and can vary from situation to situation. I feel confident in my abilities to get up in front of a room and do public speaking. For me, that is not problem. I have self-confidence in that area. I would have no self-confidence in my ability to publicly attempt complicated math problems.

Self-esteem is how you view yourself overall, in general, in all areas of your life. I've had low self-esteem when it comes to how I look. I am not supermodel material, which our American culture seems to prize. As I've gotten older, I've learned how to combat those specific Trolls more efficiently and I've chosen to care less about what people think of how I look. (See example above regarding the purple sweater.)

Make sure you have a handle on those thing in which you have self-confidence. Make a list. Write down all the things in your life, big and small, that you *know* you can do; the ones where the Trolls usually don't bother to come out. Make another list where the Trolls have a Field Day with picnic lunches, blankets, hacky-sack; they fucking bring their Troll-dogs... You get the picture. Compare the two lists and think about what on the second list needs to be reinforced. Do you need to spend more time learning how to change a flat tire? How important is that to you to know or do you just buy Road Side Assistance? Personally, I don't like being ignorant about things that are important to me so I seek out information and learn how to do stuff.

Figure that out and then work on these things, little by little. It feels good to *know*, ya know?

STEP #8: OBSESS MUCH?

> "What fascinates me about addiction and obsessive behavior is that people would choose an altered state of consciousness that's toxic and ostensibly destroys most aspects of your normal life, because for a brief moment you feel okay." ~Moby

The whole first part of this is an anecdote. Settle in, people.

Remember that shitty neighbor I have that I call Harvey? He's really just deplorable; doesn't seem to be a nice guy, at least not to those of us that live in this house. I once called around to get some quotes for new windows for the house. This guy came out to give me an estimate and as we were sitting at the kitchen table going over The Numbers (cue ominous music), he looks out the side window at Harvey's house and says, "I think I know that place. The house looks really familiar." He thinks for a minute and then realizes that he put the storm doors on or something, I really wasn't listening because I didn't care until he said,"Yeah! That's ol' Harvey's house. I love that guy. He's a laugh-riot. So fucking funny and just a great guy." That snapped me back to reality. A great guy? Really? Huh. That's not the Harvey I know. Needless to say, I did not hire that guy to do my windows.

Our place has a big-ish backyard for a city lot and we have a small fire pit in the backyard, which is totally legal. I know this because of all the firemen that have been by to check it out have told me so. Relaxing on a summer evening with a nice beverage around a small fire, chatting with friends or watching the kids catch fireflies can be such a lovely thing to do.

But then there's Harvey and he likes to fuck that shit up. "There will be no joy in my vicinity!" Harvey seems to say.

Every time we light the fire pit, he calls the police and the fire department. Every. Time. He claims it bothers him and fills his house with smoke. I can build a relatively smoke-free fire and the wood we have piled up from the two large trees that were removed from our property have been sitting there for years, not being burnt, being seasoned by the sun and the rain. That shit burns clean and it burns fast, yet ol' Harvey complains every time. The people across the street can have a fire. The people on the other side can have one, too. But not us. This is the least of what Harvey does. The list goes on but this part isn't about that.

This part is about those times we've had "words" with Harvey over his antics. I don't usually back down from a confrontation. I'm rather wee and this in itself usually puts the other person at a disadvantage because they are not expecting little wee me to turn into a ferocious mongoose but it can happen. So Harvey will start his shit and start calling us all sorts of lovely names; you know, the usual: bitch, whore, cunt, stupid bitch, piece of shit. He once called my son a bastard within ear shot of my son, he's called my husband a bisexual but we're still trying to figure out how that is an insult. Mostly he yells the traditional insults about women at me and most of the time I say nothing back. He's usually not worth me getting my adrenaline all pumping and ready for a physical fight that never happens. After the adrenaline is gone or the neighbor has retreated to his home, I think of an amazing array of clever, witty and really cut-down-to-the-bone things to say.

Back in Step #4 Stop Taking Things So Fucking Personally, I mentioned Harvey and said that he seems to have this deep and nuanced fantasy about what goes on over here and making my life miserable. Here's my hypothesis on what I think may have happened to get Harvey to this point. When I moved in to this house, it was just me and my son. I was alone, no man. I think Harvey saw this and thought, "DIBS!" and that's as far as it went. I moved in to the house in December and people are not out much, chatting over the fence in December. It wasn't until the next spring that I had any conversations with him and those were new-neighbor-friendly at best. The house I bought was in disrepair and the yard was a disaster, lots of invasive plants and had been neglected. He said, "You've got your work cut out for you over there" and proceeded to tell me about the prior residents and how horrible they were. They threw loud parties all the time, shattered glass beer bottles into the fire pit, and indeed there were layers and layers of broken glass I needed to excavate and were generally just raging hooligans. Apprantly, my house was Shenanigan Central.

The thing that tipped me off was that he gave me a circular saw. I already had one and I said as much, but he gave it to me anyway, insisted that I take it because he didn't need it and he thought I could use it. Men usually don't give gifts of any kind to women they don't like-like, ya know? I might be making a generalization but for the guys reading this, think about your own gift-giving habits. When was the last time you gave a gift of any value, of any sort, to a woman or man that you had zero interest in at all? Uh-huh. That's what I thought. I refused this circular saw but yet he just insisted, and I thought, "fuck..." Never did Harvey invite me out, invite me over, or make any overture at all that he had intentions.

Four and a half months after I moved in to my house, I met my now husband. We started dating in April. I'm pretty sure that Harvey saw Steve coming and going from the house and this fucked with his fantasy. I'm fairly certain that Harvey created some sort of fantasy relationship that included me in some way and Steve totally fucking mentally cock blocked him. Well, to Harvey, this falsely perceived aggression will not stand, man, yet Harvey did nothing about it because Harvey is really a coward when it comes to these things. In a way, I feel sad for that. We all want to be loved and cared for, cherished and adored. Being too afraid or self-conscious to reach out to someone for fear of rejection must be lonely, indeed.

I haven't talked to Harvey in any meaningful way because I can't. There is no conversation, there is only aggression and insults. There is just this fantasy that precludes anything meaningful taking place. Anything real would interfere with Harvey being the star of his fantasy story because in reality, Harvey and I would not be together. That just wasn't ever going to happen anyway and well, that would be a very difficult thing for Harvey to handle so instead it is easier and safer for Harvey to have this fantasy that he lives in where he is the hero in all matters.

What fucked up Harvey's fantasy is when I knocked on his front door and asked him quite politely to let his dog inside because it was just standing on the porch barking at the side door. From my kitchen window to his side door is about 25 feet. That's close. I work from home and my house has no air conditioning. At the time, I just worked at the kitchen table and on this particular day, I had the window open but even if the window was shut, the dog was close enough and barking loud enough to be a nuisance through the glass. Having a dog, who was very sweet and very old, barking incessantly at the door to his house a mere 20 feet from me for close to an hour was very difficult to deal with. Instead of being a bitch and calling the cops, I just went and knocked on his door. He saw me through the window and said, "Get the fuck off my porch, bitch." What was the first thing I thought? My first thought was "Wow, he's having a bad day" and then followed that with "Yeah, well could you let [dog's name] in? He's been barking at the door for a long time." His response was along the lines of "I said, 'get the fuck off my porch', you stupid bitch" blah blah blah. My knocking on his door was all that he required for him to unleash his fury and vitriol he'd built up in his mind over our 'failed relationship'.

I did call the cops and ask them to come out and intervene. Normally, I would just approach on my own and try to work it out but there was, and currently is, no 'working it out with Harvey'. He refuses to be reasonable. He is so deep in this fantasy of me having done him wrong by choosing Steve over him when there was never any choice to be made. There wasn't ever anything there. It was all crafted in his mind. It is a fucking fantasy that is having real world consequences. This is the kind of shit that could end up on the evening news. "Quiet neighbor who kept to himself fucking loses his shit and shoots up his neighbor's house." My family and friends were worried that that's how this was going to go.

An ex-parte restraining order was had and Harvey seemed smart enough to understand what all that meant. Once the ex-parte was converted to a Civil Protection Order, Harvey cut the shit. He would still flip me off or make lewd sexual gestures at me, which was not covered in the CPO and might be protected by the 1st amendment anyway. The CPO expired and I tried to get it renewed but the judge wanted video and audio proof of continued harassment, which I tried to get but Harvey, again, would cut the shit any time I tried to get him on video. He ain't stupid, just fucked in the head.

One of the solutions to this problem and the one Harvey would love, would be for us to move. Granted, our house is a little small for four people and a plethora of cats but we have a nice big yard for plants and a garden, which, oh yeah, Harvey will spray if anything is along the fence line. The trees Harvey hated so much were cut down, one more to go, and the wood was stacked up along the property line on his side. That's as much vengeance as I can muster. I really just have better things to do with my time than spend it trying to figure out ways to fuck with Harvey.

It has been five years. I have no current CPO against Harvey but he seems to have chilled a bit. In the summertime, last year I did try to avoid being in the backyard at the same time Harvey was outside. I would very much like to move my side door to the back of house where I makes far more sense. Who the fuck thought up this house's layout anyway? Fuckwad. I avoid him when I can and I protect my children if they are outside when he is out with his new dog. I don't engage but I don't back down. Oh, yeah, he and his adult child accused me of killing their dogs. I fucking *love* dogs, even theirs. His new dog is just the fucking cutest pittie ever. I want to squeeze his little face. Just...the shit is so fucked up. Anyway, I don't seek out confrontation with him but I won't back down if he starts his shit up again.

Point of that really fucking long anecdote?

Do not live in your fantasies. They are not fucking real. If this fantasy shit gets out of control, then bad things can happen. Harvey has not tried to physically hurt me but isn't it sad to think that the cops can do nothing for me until he does? The judge stated what she needed to extend the CPO and Harvey has avoided these things. Maybe this is enough of a deterrent. For other people, though, maybe it is not.

Life is out here. Not in your phone. Not in your head. Not on a screen. It is out here with us, in the shit. Life can get shitty and that fucking sucks but we all have to wade through that shit and come out the other side, more the wiser. We can all be our own worst critics. I know I can be. I'm pretty good at beating myself up sometimes but then I remember that I wouldn't say that shit about most people, save Harvey. Even with him, I still have compassion because he must feel crushing loneliness. I can chew on the cud of a mistake for a week or more, but to what end? What good does it do me to obsess over something like a fuck up or a flippant comment? It does me no good at all. I can attempt atonement and ask for forgiveness, make it right somehow then move the fuck on.

Obsessing over all sorts of things leads nowhere but down a rabbit hole of despair, right to The Edge of The fucking Abyss. If you find that you might have OCD or any other legit illness that results in obsessive behaviors or thoughts that are causing all sorts of real world problems, seek some help. You need to get that shit straight. Anything that might consume your time in its entirety is not good and not healthy. For me, this is especially concerning when it is obsession with other people. Again I say that I am not an expert in psychiatry or mental illness but I have been both obsessed with someone and been on the receiving end of obsession and none of it feels good and in the case of being obsessed with people, can be illegal.

If you find yourself obsessed with another person and that person is in no way reciprocating any sort of affection or attention, stop beating yourself up and look around. There might be someone else *right there* waiting for you to get out of your head and notice that they are there. Didn't Taylor Swift write a song about that?

We all learn through trial and error. We learn by doing, then fucking it up, and then hopefully learning that that wasn't the way to do it and so the next time, you don't do *that* and instead try something else. When shit goes haywire, and it will, that doesn't make you scum on the bottom of your shoe, it makes you human.

Go ahead and look forward to the next party with friends, or that night out with your sweetie, or the cool trip you are about to go on, or whatever life event you have coming up. That's great. I wish I was going on a cool trip.

Just remember: You cannot live there. You cannot live where the grass is greener because the grass you have is just as good, you need only tend to it a bit more. The problem with this way of thinking is that you end up wishing your life away and didn't we already go over all this?

SECTION 3: PROCRASTINATING

> "Being busy is a form of laziness - lazy thinking and indiscriminate actions. Being busy is most often used as a guise for avoiding the few critically important but uncomfortable actions." ~ Tim Ferriss

Put the smart phone down, unless you are reading this on one then don't. But yeah, put the fucking thing down. NOW.

Procrastination is something that we all do, even the wee ones and much like the situation with money, if you don't know where you are spending your time, you can't really fix the problems that come with time wasting. And, I know that it feels like you have all your fucking life to accomplish something but take it from me: that time will go by quickly and the time you think you had will be gone and your future is Now and you got nuttin' to show for it. I know this feeling all too well. I really have a hard time believing sometimes that the nineties weren't just a few years ago. They were two fucking decades ago, soon to be three. When I think about this, I say, "Where the fuck did the time go?"

I pissed it away, that's where it went.

Just pissed it away, down The Drain of Fucking Off, of not knowing what I wanted, of thinking that I had an unlimited amount of Laters. I can tell you what I want now: I want all those previous Nows back.

I think that the vast majority of us waste time because we don't want to attempt whatever it is that is critically important, according to Tim F., and that it might hurt. Also, aside from being uncomfortable as stated above, we might be embarrassed by our lack of skill in the thing we are trying to do. Fear of failure is a great motivator to procrastinate.

"Well, if I don't try then I can't say that I failed."

Hells bells. I'm in college at 47. I thought I did the reading. I thought I understood it. I took the quiz on the material. I got every fucking question wrong. I completely failed that shit.

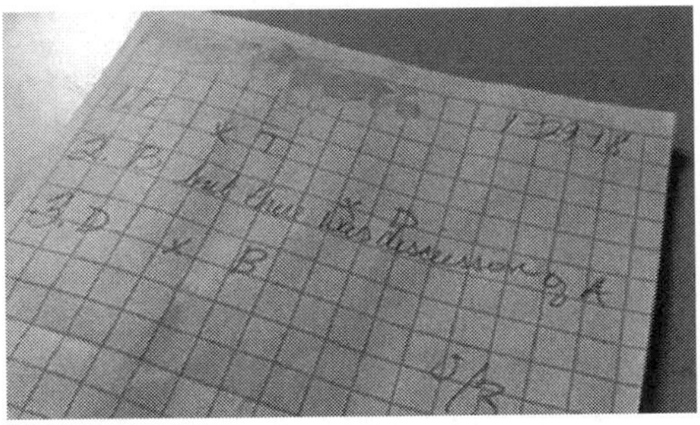

Oopsie...

Apparently, I didn't do the reading close enough. I didn't quit school. I didn't burn it all to the ground. I did feel bad for a bit because I really did think I understood what I read. All that big fat zero told me was that I didn't do the work well enough. Sure, I *failed.* No biggie. My self-worth isn't wrapped up in a single three question quiz about some reading assignment. I will read the next assignment with more of a critical eye. Also, I won't lie: when I pop into my online student interface and I see my current grade for that class hovering at a low C because of the quiz, I get a little twitchy... then I think, "Well, Cs get degrees and Elon Musk doesn't care about college degrees anyway." Then I go back to being awesome.

The feelings of procrastination have sprung up, though. I know there is another reading and probably another bullshit quiz and there is a little Troll in me that says, "Fuck the readings. Fuck the teacher. Fuck it all!! Go write instead. Or play that stupid game on your phone." I can think of a million trillion things I could do instead of the stupid readings.

Yet.

I must be done.

Eyes on the Prize, people.

STEP 9: STOP FUCKING DOING NOTHING.

> "Don't let the fear of the time it will take to accomplish something stand in the way of your doing it. The time will pass anyway; we might just as well put that passing time to the best possible use." ~ Earl Nightingale

You do realize that all of this up until now has really just been a really fucking elaborate way for y'all to procrastinate, right?

I could just stop right the hell here and tell you to read two books and wrap this shit up. The two books I would highly suggest you read are "The 4-Hour Work Week" by the above-mentioned Tim Ferriss and the other is "The 80/20 Principle" by Richard Koch. I don't expect you to do what Tim did in his book but it is a master class in being fucking focused as shit and getting your shit done. The other is about the Pareto principle, that the vast majority of your results, 80%, can and probably do come from about 20% of your effort. Go ahead and read those two books. I'll wait.

That's the great thing about books. I can just sit here and wait, indefinitely. I'm not going anywhere. It's lovely.

◆ ◆ ◆

I'm going to assume that you didn't read those books like I told you to and that you procrastinated the shit out of that, too. For fuck's sake.

E.B. is disappointed in you.

Let me ask you a question: how much fucking time do you think you have? If you are 20-something, you probably think that you have all the fucking time in the world. No hurry. Just like when you were a kid.

If you are older than 35, I ask you to seriously think about how long ago being 21 was. Felt like yesterday, didn't it?

On my 3am days, the ones where I get up to write essentially in the middle of the night, I look in the bathroom mirror and for a brief moment, I think, "Who the fuck is that?" I point and look around to see if anyone else is seeing what I'm seeing. No one else is even up at this ridiculous hour, but what I see in the mirror is not the E.B. I see in my head. I stopped aging at 32 in my head but the mirror tells a different story. Where the fuck did all that time go and what the hell do I have to show for it?

You don't have as much time as you think you do and yet, you have all the time in the world. It is such a fucking paradox.

So, which is it, E.B., all the time in the world or no time at all?

Both.

You have both.

In the moment you are in, right now, is all the time in the world. You only ever have the Now. You have it solidly and it is not going anywhere. You have to be in the Now now, not later because Later doesn't exist. At least not to humans. It might all exist at once and already be gone but we have to move through space in a fucking straight-ass linear manner. We as humans don't yet have the capacity to be everywhere and every-when all at once. You have Now. That's it. Fucking Carpe Diem, ya know? That's what that shit means. Time is just a series of Nows lined up one right after the other and it feels like some of the Nows don't matter. If one of those Nows is standing around in a queue waiting for a Later that's not yet a Now, then do something productive with that Now.

I hear the argument: I can't possibly be doing something productive for every single fucking waking moment to make the most of every Now that I have. And to that I say, then what are you doing with your Nows most of the time? Be honest with yourself. Do you find that you are procrastinating most of the time because you might be afraid of something else?

Quick tangent. One of my personal heroes is Amelia Earhart. She was hard core awesome and a true pioneer in female aviation at at time when women were just not supposed to do those things. I find her endlessly fascinating but what I'd like to bring up is something that she is quoted as saying "Courage is the price life exacts for granting peace."

Let's dwell on that for a minute. Just one Now.

If you want some peace in your life regarding some *thing* that you want to do, then you have to have the courage to actually do it. You have to have the courage to go through the previous steps, or at least the ones you think you need to go through, you may not need to go through them all, just to get to the point where you have the courage to do your *thing*.

Courage, as defined by the dictionary, is "...the ability to do something that frightens one." Shit gets scary, yo. I get that but you have a few choices. You can either do nothing, which I would prefer you stop doing, or you can do it and still be afraid.

"Courage (having the fear and doing it anyway) is the price (what you have to sacrifice) life exacts (really living) for granting peace (having no regrets)."

I'm willing to sacrifice my fear to really live my life and have no regrets as I die, whenever that ends up being.

Are you?

You have Now so do something with it, for fuck's sake.

Email? It can wait.

Your phone? Put that dastardly machine down. Better yet, give it to a toddler and you'll never see the fucking thing again. It is like they have their own personal black holes that they just throw your shit into and it never reappears. Toddlers are really great at losing your shit. Just give something to them and it will disappear in a matter of seconds never to be seen again. Or if it does come back, it won't be the same. It'll have gray hair and a wild look in its eyes because it has seen some serious shit you would never believe... that's where your stuff goes when you give it to a toddler. What the fuck?

The dishes? Eh. They can wait, too. Or if you have a kid, teach them how to do it and then when you need to be productive, you can just point at them and say, "Do it." Problem solved. If you don't have a kid, fucking put your dish in the damned dishwasher the minute you finish with the thing. The dish's final destination is back in the cupboard, all nice and clean and whereas you don't have to do that, at least get it to a stopping point. Rinse it off and stack it for later or put it in the dishwasher if you have one. Be courteous but don't let that override your need to do important things.

Anything else you deem more important in your life at that moment that will keep you from doing the really important work?

Fuck it. Fuck it for Now.

Tim's quote up there is spot-fucking-on. I see this in my kid. I ask him to brush his teeth every night before bed. Every night. The child is 8 years old, so let's consider that he was able to brush his own teeth reliably from the age of, say, 5, on, with minimal supervision from me. That's just over a thousand times that he's done it. Wouldn't you think that with that amount of repetition he'd know to just fucking brush his teeth before bed without me having to ask him and, more importantly, that he'd realize that it ain't no big deal and to just fucking do it and get it done?

Nope.

Every night, he procrastinates. He finds all kinds of very important things to do on his way to the bathroom to complete a two-minute task.

"Go brush your teeth now, please"
"But I have to pet the cats. All of them." We have five and they like to hide. Specifically, from him.
"Just go. Now. Brush your teeth."
"But there is this book I need to look at."

Oh, for fuck's sake, really? I give him The Stare.

"Look, Mom! There's fuzz on the floor." I'm not kidding he said that on his way to the bathroom once, it was probably cat hair from him giving the cats too much "love", and felt that at that moment, the most important thing in his life was to clean that fuzz in the hallway but fuck all if I ask him to clean his room. Ain't nobody got time for that. To an eight-year-old, those two minutes of teeth brushing feel like a lifetime spent doing something shitty. He doesn't know that good dental hygiene is the gateway to good health. He doesn't realize that two minutes really isn't that long.

Conversely, you might think, "Oh, I'll just pop on to [favorite social media, news or website] for a few minutes. I need a breather."

<TWO HOURS LATER>

You look up from your phone or tablet or laptop and realize that it wasn't a few minutes, it was *hours*. You spent hours doing ... what exactly? What did you get out of that? If you were learning, researching, exploring and using that information to better yourself, fine... But now let's talk about how you can justify and rationalize the shit out of your bad behavior so that you don't have to feel bad for fucking off for all your allotted time. The Internet is going to be there when you get done with your important work. The news will still be there and it'll probably be more of the same anyway.

Watch for this shitty behavior in yourself. The only way you are going to successfully remove your head from your ass in any kind of permanent way is to be aware of it in yourself. Not that you exist, "I am here." Yeah, we know. We see you, but do you know you are here and what you are doing or thinking at any given moment? Where's your head at? Are you able to discern where your head is mentally or what your body is doing at that moment to be able to circumvent the actions? Can you stop yourself?

Yes, you can and you'd fucking better.

One of the phrases that people say that I can't stand is: "I can't."

◆ ◆ ◆

Anecdote Time!

Remember when I said that I'd moved to Los Angeles rather abruptly when I was 35 and my mother was pissed? I moved to LA with a guy I really hadn't been dating all that long. He ended up being a royal fucking prick but that's a story for another time. He was working on a career in cinematography and got a job on a film once we were in LA. I'm fairly certain that 85% of the shit he ever said to me was a lie in some capacity so suffice it to say that he got "hurt" on the set of this film. He spun me some tale about how he was trying to raise up a huge light on set with another guy and it was slipping or some shit and blah blah blah, he torqued his shoulder and he couldn't work. Maybe he was hurt enough to not work for a little bit but whatever. Once he was home to recuperate, he did nothing around the house. He didn't cook a meal, he didn't wash a dish, he didn't pick up anything. He wouldn't do laundry. He did fucking nothing. It was fucking infuriating. Again, I don't like people who don't contribute when they are perfectly capable of doing so. But, "he was hurt!" you say, and to that I say he wasn't *that* hurt.

We were watching a feel-good news story about a woman with no arms who had a baby and how she managed to take care of this little one with no arms. That would seem like a basic requirement, to have arms to carry, feed, change the baby but this woman, and many others like her, do it without any arms. She was fucking amazing. I don't remember her name and if she was an LA native or what but that what she was doing was mind-blowing. I watched this story and I was in awe of her. I thought, "that woman doesn't let anything stop her. The words 'I can't' don't exist to her. She's my new hero." I said something to Royal Fucking Prick about her. I said, "Look at that! She's taking care of a baby with no arms and yet here you are with a perfectly good arm and one slightly bum shoulder and you are doing nothing, not even the laundry." He responded with "I'm too hurt to do the laundry." He could have dragged the laundry bag down the hall to the laundry room but no. He wasn't that kind of guy. He was a Royal Fucking Prick with a bum shoulder and fuck all if he was going to do anything. He said "I can't." not because he couldn't but because he didn't want to.

◆ ◆ ◆

Be honest with yourself. You are probably more fucking capable than you realize and yet you continuously tell yourself that you can't.

Can't.

Fuck that shit.

You don't *want* to.

Why don't you want to? Because you might 'fail', whatever that means?

All right. Don't, then. Don't fucking do anything and then don't complain any about anything either. Let's all cue up Gandhi and remember that you need to be the change you wish to see in the world. Your world. If you want something different, then the words "I can't" need to disappear from your vocabulary. Kick the I Can't Troll to the fucking curb and run it over with your mental Mac truck. Just fucking get rid of those words and the Trolls they rode in on.

You can; you're just being a lazy fuckhead.

Stop it.

Give your phone to the nearest toddler and go focus on your shit.

Go get that shit done.

Now.

Go.

For fuck's sake, it's like telling my kid to brush his teeth.

Fuck the fuzz, get your shit done Now.

STEP 10: TICK TOCK, MOTHER FUCKERS.

> "If time be of all things the most precious, wasting time must be the greatest prodigality." ~Benjamin Franklin

Getting back to the sense of not having any time. What is filling your time? Oh, wait, have you ever done a budget? No?

Fuckhead.

When you read or learn from any kind of money master, they will tell you that the first thing you need to do is audit your money and discover where it is going so that you know where to plug the leaks. Sounds legit, right? Yeah, very few people actually do this. Why?

"I can't."

No. Fuck that. You don't **want** to because you don't want to know the truth. You don't want your illusions that someone else is taking your money or that you don't make enough (which is probably true but again, for another time) to smash into the reality that you're straight up shitty with money. You don't want to face that so you are not doing the work to figure out what the problem is.

Ignorance is bliss, right?

Fuckhead.

Add ignorance to the list of things I can't stand. If you know that you don't know, then go learn. Inside your fucking skull is a pretty kick-ass computer-like thingy called your brain. Go use the fucking thing.

If you have done a budget. Good for you. I won't call you a fuckhead right now and you can have a cookie. When you did said budget, did it show you that you spent way too much money on porn? Or Starbucks? Or comics? Or comics about porn at Starbucks? Oh, never mind. Porn is free on the Internet. Did you realize that you were doing that? If you didn't realize you were doing that, were you shocked at your own behavior and set about rectifying said behavior? No?

Fuckhead.

Change is hard. No one is going to tell you it isn't but yet you have to think about the potential outcome of the work of doing a time budget or a budget-budget or anything else worth doing. How will you benefit if you complete the work? Is that worth the short-term inconvenience and discomfort of going through change? Is it worth not knowing every single thing that happened on social media while you were working to better yourself? I think it is and you should, too.

People say, "I have no time." Uh huh. Right. I don't believe you. We all have the same amount of time in each day unless you have access to some time portal and in that case, none of this applies to you. If you have a T.A.R.D.I.S. I politely request being able to check that shit out.

◆ ◆ ◆

Anecdote Time!

I found myself gainfully unemployed around 2001. This was right before I was hired on a crew that worked as maintenance for a set of apartments, which was my job, and then branched into doing home remodeling. Seriously. I have pictures. I have proof.

Anyway, I was unemployed for about three months and living on savings. I didn't have much in the way of bills. I had a little dog at the time named Ike, as well as Jenna the German Shepherd, and he liked to hop around on his back paws. This, of course, meant that he absolutely *needed* to have a fez. This started me down a path of "I don't have time for a job." I ended up making him a fez. It was quite elaborate. I made it from a Dixie cup and some felt, a small tassel, some rick rack and elastic. I still have it. Other dogs have worn it. Soon, I was able to fill my time with all sorts of essentially meaningless activities that didn't get me anywhere. There was creative satisfaction that was being had, that was nice, but I wasn't making anything of myself. I wasn't advancing myself. The money ran out and I had to find work quickly.

◆◆◆

There was this pervasive feeling of not having any time. I was able to fill my time with so much meaninglessness that it really did feel like I didn't have anything left. I felt that all the things I was doing were equally important and therefore demanded my time. This was before Facebook or any major social media inventions, around 2003. To me I had very important priorities, where on earth would I find time for a job?

I had to shift my priorities. I had to decide what was *more* important, you know, the basic shit like housing and feeding myself.

Our current world is filled with so many fucking distractions. They are everywhere. I leave my phone on silent almost all the time. I don't even like to hear it beep or buzz. There are times when I will put it on vibrate so that I can take the call I am expecting or respond to the text I am waiting for but after that, it goes back to silent. I do not let it, that stupid little machine, dictate what I do with my time. I cannot. Not if I want to make something of myself and be better.

That little fucker can fuck the fuck off.

Television, music, the Internet, newspapers and magazines, even *gasp*, books can all be distracting and ways to waste time instead of doing the work that needs to be done.

You have the time until you don't and you won't realize that you no longer have the time until it is gone. In the last section, I mentioned how I sometimes grab a quick view of myself in the mirror and I think, "*Who* is that?" The mental construct I have of myself right now is the one of me when I was in my early to mid-thirties. That was a great time in my life and for a bit, I think I've stopped there to dwell mentally. My body was in great shape, I was making okay money but it was just me and the dog and cat, I was doing some film-making, having a good time...most of the time...with my friends. It was a wonderful time in my life so my mental construct is stuck there for a while.

However, I am so far past that point, like 15 years past that point. It is time for me to move my mental construct forward and over the last few years it is has shifted. The reason why is because those fifteen years went lightning fast. My nephew just turned fourteen. We were over at my brother's house for a family party; you know, the usual: cake, ice cream, mud, crying, slamming door, etc. Anyway, we were having our cake and I said to the birthday boy, "Weren't we *just* here at a birthday party for you?" and he looked at me kinda funny as he laughed and he said "Yeah, but that was last year." I said, "Last year felt like last month. You're turning fourteen today, but you'll be 21 by the end of the week according to the clock in my head." Then I saw him at the surprise party my new sister-in-law had for my brother. My nephew comes up to me to say hi and said, "Hey, didn't you hear?" I shook my head because I didn't know what he was referencing. He said, "I just turned 21!" My brother and his eldest son's birthdays are eight days apart. My nephew is adorable and funny; both of them are.

If you are reading this as a young man or woman, time fucking flies and it flies faster and faster the older you get. When I was in my early 20s, I squandered all kinds of time because I felt like I had *decades* to do something with myself then I grab a view of myself in the mirror and think, "Shit, those decades came and went and what the fuck was I doing with myself?" A good portion of that answer could be the basis of another book but suffice it to say that I felt like I had all the time in the world but what I was doing was wasting all that time on what is discussed in all the previous chapters. I put this one last because whereas it might seem like a good place to start, it is actually the best place to end.

I didn't understand the concept of the Now. I was only focused on the Later. I wasn't in the moment I was in but wishing, hoping, daydreaming about the Later, while casting blame backwards towards others. I blamed others for my past and future but I wasn't ever really in the Now. Twenty some odd years of learning to get to this point. I'm in the second half of my life and I've just now learned all these lessons. One of the things I don't do very much of because I cannot afford it, is to What If myself. "What if I had learned all these lessons before I left high school? What brilliances could I have achieved? What magical things could I have done?" This is all just fantasy and daydreams. Maybe I could go back through and re-live my life as a "Choose Your Own Adventure" book but to what end? I can't go back and change anything. Again, unless one of you has a T.A.R.D.I.S, then maybe I could but all those movies we've seen about changing the space time continuum has taught us that that is a very bad idea.

My life has made me who I am up to this point. Since I cannot go back and change it, I can only use the experiences as reference points ("Learning experiences!" I hear my mother saying) to be able to move forward through my successive Nows to achieve goals. I can honestly say as well that I had no clearly defined goals in my early adult years. I had no idea what I wanted because I was still working on some other things that should have happened or been learned when I was a teenager. This is where I would start blaming my parents and things come full circle and we are back at the beginning. I don't blame them anymore. Thankfully, we live in a time when people are living longer and longer. I am taking care of myself better and I have plans to live another 50 fully functioning years.

I can hear the collective groaning of the younger set, "...but I'm only 20. I have *plenty* of time." No. You don't. That's what I am trying to tell you, mother fuckers. You don't have as much time as you think you do. If you are in your twenties, then one year of your life is only about 5% of its total. That can feel like a long time and since you haven't lived past that age, you can't see that each successive year actually becomes less of a percentage of your total life. Life is fucking logarithmic, yo, not linear. Didn't I say this already? Each year that you live becomes less of the total of your life, collectively. This is why that one glorious summer spent at that resort in the hills learning to dance with that hot guy, feels like it lasted forever.[1] Percentage-wise, in the totality of your life, it did, but now, as you age, those years become less and less of the total and each one goes whizzing the fuck by you as if to say, "Later, losers!"

The procrastinating and the living in the fucking past and the daydreaming and social media... it all just steals your life away. If I could grab you all by your lapels and shake you back and forth while gritting my teeth and snarling at you: YOU DO

NOT HAVE THE TIME. I told you go to read Tim Ferriss' book The 4-Hour Work Week. I told you that was a master class in how to make the most use of your time. I strongly encourage you to go and get the book. Actually, read every fucking thing Tim Ferriss has ever written. That man is brilliant.

I like my sleep. Naps are totally wasted on toddlers. I want nothing more than to go to bed, in my own bed since I am a very light sleeper, in my very dark and quiet room and sleep until I naturally wake up. That could be 6 hours, that could be 10 hours. I would love that. This is not to be, not at this point in my life. I'm going to go on a slight tangent for a second but trust me, it'll all come back around to time.

There are literally thousands of online gurus of all makes and models selling whatever program they have developed to "help you get the life you want." There is usually some really long-winded video presentation that is free and promises to give you the 3 weird tricks to making money online and financial freedom. If you have Internet access then you have seen these folks. I have bought some social media marketing courses, how to leverage your presence online and stuff like that. There was one course that was really well done and had a ton of great information that was truly useful and I felt it was money well spent. Of course, I then get an email from that producer about a 'friend' of hers that was making a ton of money online by doing these "3 weird tricks" and she wanted to let me know about her 'friend'. The friend had a free 1-hour video class that was nothing more than the loss leader to her more expensive courses and programs.

I click on the link...wait, should there be an "Anecdote time!" right here? Regardless, I started to watch the first video and it was overwhelmingly selling a daydream. Of the total 1 hour of free video, there was actually only about 5 minutes of truly useful information. The rest was selling a dream. This video was all about how she used to be almost homeless in one of the most expensive cities in the country with three kids after a nasty divorce and now wakes up whenever she wants with the ocean breezes wafting gently through her gauzy white curtains. She leisurely goes about her morning, savoring her first cup of coffee out on the deck that overlooks the Pacific Ocean while watching her well-adjusted non-emo teen-aged children cavorting in the surf and on the beach. Eventually, she will make her way to her office and spend whatever minimal amount of time on her business and will passively earn some ridiculous number of dollars. All of this imagery was shown. She was wearing a great outfit in a wonderfully decorated office/studio. The fantasy was fantastic.

Don't get me wrong, I love a good rags-to-riches story and I would very much like to be a rags-to-riches story but what I found most distasteful about her videos, well,

I found a lot of things distasteful but the one thing that stood out the most was that she seemed to be saying that you wouldn't really have to do much and that it wouldn't take up much of your *time*. I know it was just a sales pitch, a great a story that would hook someone to click the "BUY NOW" button. I get that. I've studied online marketing. I understand that part of it but I wouldn't want to knowingly mislead anyone about the realities of it all. Andrew Carnegie said it first, I think, and my mother repeated it endlessly and again, as she was saying it, I was rolling my teen-aged eyes as far back into my head as humanly possible and groaning but it is true: Anything in life worth having is worth *working* for.

You have to work, fucksticks.

You are not getting out of that.

Unless someone hands you 10 million dollars and tells you to go buy yourself something nice and not to spend it all in one place, you are going to have to work for it. There will have to be effort and effort takes time. I liked that video's daydream. I would love to wake up whenever the fuck I wanted in a beach house with gentle ocean breezes wafting gently through my gauzy curtains. I would love to have my morning cup of coffee on my kick ass deck overlooking the Pacific Ocean, or any ocean that's warm, more specifically. There is nothing wrong with that daydream. If that is the goal, then going back to the very beginning of this fucking book, it needs to be written down as the goal and a plan to get it needs to be made. Then...uh, what's that? Oh, yes, time. Time will need to be spent to achieve the goal.

If you want your mutha-fucking coffee on your mutha-fucking deck overlooking the mutha-fucking ocean[2] and someone has not given you all those things, you might actually have to spend the time to work for it. You have to work and work takes time. All of these video courses and online get-rich-quick schemes are really selling that: how to keep your time for yourself and not spend it working. Even Tim's book is called The 4-Hour Work Week but that was the end result, that is **not** where you start. You never start out just working four hours a week to make a shit-ton of money. It says it right there but the hook is that you will do this is in "15 minutes! That's it!" or "four hours a week!" or "I spend just two hours a day on my business and rake in thousands per hour." Any iteration of this theme is out there. We all know that time is money and that all things really come down to one of those things. You either don't have enough time or enough money and with someone like me, you might not have much of both.

This is where sleep comes in. I told you it would come back around. I like my sleep but sleep is the one place where I can spare a little time. I already have silver hair and bags under my eyes, missing a few hours of sleep isn't going to hurt too much if I don't do it for too long. I have been getting up early, like I said, 3:30am, to come to my desk and write. Every day. Except Friday of last week and this past Monday. Friday, I got up to write and we've all had these days, I just couldn't make the magic happen. I ended up laying down for a tick on the small Ikea couch near my desk, my sweet tiny black kitty, Ziva, joined me and I zonked out for another hour. Oops. Then, this past Monday, in the middle of the night, I woke up enough to proclaim to the cat that was on the bed with me, probably Bonbon, that I was officially sick. My question is why sickness, like a head cold or whatever, can hit you like a fucking truck and you'll declare that you are officially sick but why can't it leave the same way? Why can't all the viruses just die at once and you can quickly proclaim "I am no longer sick!" That would be fantastic. Suffice it to say that I spent Monday in bed. I got the boy on the bus, the baby, although she would tell you that she's a li'l girl, not a baby, to the daycare provider then I said to myself, "Self, you are going to go home and sleep for one and one-half hours. You will then rise up and go to lecture. Henceforth from lecture, you will carefully procure the youngest child from the daycare provider and proceed home to greet the boy upon his return from his educational establishment. Dinner will be made, probably by you, and a lovely evening will ensue." Yeah, none of that happened. I had the nothing but the noblest intentions for all of that and I did go home and sleep for one and one-half hours; I woke up only long enough to send a quick email to my professor and TA that I was sick in bed. When my husband came home from work around 2pm, he saw I was still in bed and had this look about him that was less "Oh, she's sick. That sucks for her" and more "Oh, she's sick. Fuck, I have to do everything now?!" I kid, I kid. He did run point on parenting until the next day. He carefully procured the youngest from the daycare provider, greeted the boy and made them all dinner. I laid in bed and groaned.

My point is that I am up, every day, at my desk no later than 4am and I write. I don't surf the Internet, I don't look at Facebook, I fucking don't look at my emails and I don't dick around with games. I sit here and I write. Sometimes it is good and sometimes it is not. Some days, I proofread for typos and continuity, and laugh at my own writing in a good way, some days I just fucking hack away until something marginally workable comes out. The kids are up by 7am most days. That gives me about 3 hours of useful time to focus on my shit. I focus. I sit here and drink copious amounts of tea or coffee and I work. I sleep no more than 6 hours a night. That is the spot where I have something to give. I know it is just for now, it is not forever. I think about those ocean breezes and sitting here in the basement at a cold metal desk (that was a dumb idea, buying a metal desk to put in the basement. But it is vintage and fucking cool as shit and it still has the key!) with the space heater on and the cat, usually Ziva, on the little metal pull out shelf that is over the space heater to give her a toasty perch, drinking my coffee or tea and writing. It is not perfect. I'm not waking up whenever I want. I am not having my coffee on my deck overlooking the ocean. I have learned my lessons and I am doing the work.

Maybe someone would say that I am hustling. Over the years, I have grown less fond of that word. I am not forcing someone and I'm done with being busy for sake of busyness. Tim's quote that starts this section mentions that. I can find innumerable things around here to fill my time but when I am about to start a task that is not directly related to caring for my family, I have to ask myself some questions.

They are, in no particular order and maybe with different wording, as such:
Is this task furthering you toward achieving your goals?
Will this generate any revenue for you?
How does this help you get farther ahead tomorrow than where you are today?
Is this really the best use of the time you have right Now?
Is this really the most efficient way?
Can you teach the child to do this for future time saving?
What is the end purpose of the thing you are about to do?

If I am honest with myself about these questions and questions like them, then I find that I can easily keep myself from spending too much time on time wasters like my smartphone. I do like social media but I do not spend hours there. I post, I scroll for a bit, and then I leave. I don't scroll for hours. I don't usually surf the Internet. I read articles about current events or books on my reading app, I look things up that have come up in conversation with the kids, or I play a game to distract the children if we are waiting somewhere. Sometimes when I am waiting for the bus to get to class, because parking on campus is stupid expensive, I will want to pop onto the phone and just fuck off. I stop myself. I look up. I see what is going on around me. I am quite okay with being alone with my thoughts.

Wanna hear something that is heinous to most every person I tell? When I bought my beloved little Nissan in 2006, it had no stereo. I'm fairly convinced that the owner prior to me was a young man and he'd tried to spiff up the car a bit by putting in a stereo and crazy speakers. I bought my sweet little five speed with no stereo and I was about to drive it from Ohio to California. That trip, by car in the summer is about 3 and a half days of driving all day long. I didn't have a CD player or a smartphone or anything like that. I was just me and the road and my thoughts. Personally, I find that long distance driving with no stereo is a wonderful way to really get in touch with what is going on in my head. After about half a day of whizzing thoughts, the drone of the road calms everything down, I sincerely think it is a form of meditation for me, and my deeper mind is able to say "So, since I have you here, we need to discuss a few things." I'm a bit of a captive audience and what am I going to say to my deeper mind? "No"?

No.

I listen.
I think.
I ponder.
I take notes.

This has led me to the belief that if you are a person who cannot stand quiet or constantly needs to be stimulated, then maybe you have no desire to be alone with your own thoughts.

Time is the one thing you don't have as much of as you think you do. The way we humans process time is inconsistent. It is not the same for every minute of the day. You do have the time and you don't have the time. You have both.

Footnotes[1]

[1] This is a reference to the movie Dirty Dancing. This is not something I experienced, sadly.

[2] Didja all read that with Samuel L. Jackson's voice?

> "Enough is enough! I have had it with these mutha-fucking snakes on this mutha-fucking plane. Everybody strap in. We're about to open some fucking windows..." ~Samuel L. Jackson from the movie Snakes on a Plane

...with gauzy white curtains blowing in the gentle ocean breezes.

TIME TO WRAP THIS SHIT UP

> "Closing time...
> Every new beginning comes from some other beginning's end."
> ~Dan Wilson of Semisonic

Here is one final thing to think about before you try being an adult again. I personally don't know if you can actually get what you want without having a handle on all those things I just discussed. Even if maybe you're not an expert at any of it but at least have a general idea where your deficiencies lie and could say that you are actually aware of and working on them, is a step in the right direction.

From personal experience with a variety of people, it seems that those who knew what they wanted from a young age don't have these issues. Or, if they do have these issues, they have really good control over them.

What is all the dissatisfaction about anyway? Why don't people seem at least neutral if not somewhat happy? Much of it may have to do with expectations. So many expectations are unreasonable. If you have expectations about something or someone and it or they don't live up to those expectations, then there is going to be disappointment. Disappointment doesn't usually result is joyous celebration. It usually begets more disappointment or negative emotions, and soon there is this downward spiral. Expectations are also usually not expressed, as in "Hello. I have an expectation that you will not be a fucking dumbass. Oh, look. I've been disappointed." A quick way to avoid all of this is just to lower expectations or, better yet, have none at all. If you have no expectations, you cannot have disappointment in the thing that you didn't get because you weren't really expecting it anyway. If you do get it, huzzah!

Here's where it gets more fucked up: what if your expectations do not match your wants/needs? What if your expectations are all over the fucking map because you really have no fucking idea what it is you actually want? Let that sink in for a second. I honestly feel that the vast majority of people don't have any fucking clue what they want. They might have a pretty good idea of what they *don't* want but that's not enough. If you don't know what it is exactly that you do want but you have an idea of what you don't want, then what happens is a bunch of shit that you don't want just coming at you, and you feel barraged and, like, "What the fuck is all this shit!? I don't want any of this crap." It can be overwhelming and make it feel like you are not getting anywhere. You're just dealing with an onslaught of shit and probably distracted by a ton of shiny things.

Let's back this train the fuck up.

◆ ◆ ◆

Anecdote time!
This is a short one so no worries. When I set out to buy a house in 2012, I had very little money to do it with but I had an awesome real estate agent who really wanted to make sure I got the most for my money. She wasn't going to make much on this deal and I'm sure she didn't want to hand hold me through my first house purchase and waste a lot of her time, so her advice to me was spot on: Make a top ten list of the things the house must (or should) have in descending order of importance. For example, the first thing on the list is something the house absolutely must have, like off street parking and/or a garage, then on down the list to number 10 which would be super awesome but if it didn't have that, it'd be alright, like a linen closet. What this list did was focus the attention for both of us. At first, house hunting was a lot of fun but the novelty quickly wore off, at least it did for me and it became a chore. By having a top ten list of things, I had to really think about the kind of house I wanted, which narrowed the prospects down so that we were not traisping around to

every house in my price range. I still think we physically walked through or drove by close to 100 houses before I found the one I bought. Several were wonderful but were quickly snatched up by real estate flippers who could just drop a check or money order for the house because my price range was pretty low. The house I have now is missing two of the things on my list: a linen closet and an outdoor living space like a deck or patio. I have no linen closet and in fact, my house has very little functional storage space. I have a side door that leads out to a small porch, then there is a short path that leads around the house to the back. All of the little Cape Cod style houses in my neighborhood have these. The houses were built in the early 40s and so maybe they thought side doors would be neighborly? I'm not sure who designed this house and the ones like it but I have a huge-ass yard and no fucking back door. Who the fuck thought that was that a good idea? Fucking stupid. The point is that maybe I should have passed on this house because of that one thing. I am not happy with the fact that I don't have a back door and a deck or patio. Putting one in would require a total renovation of the kitchen, which it desperately needs. Where the back door would go is where my kitchen counter is right now. That would all have to be relocated. The thing is that the price was so fucking right, as in...stupendously inexpensive and I was able to fight to get the small mortgage and have a home instead of an apartment. So far, the trade-off has been worth it even with Harvey the Shitastic Neighbor.

By having a list of must-haves, you essentially can pare away the dead weight and focus on what you want. Do this for as many things in life as you can: a job/career, a significant other, a place to live, a car, whatever is big. I understand that sometimes you have to live a little before you can know what you want and I also understand that with jobs, there might not be a lot of choices. The thing is to not let three decades go by before you start figuring this shit out because if you do, you'll be in middle age wondering what the fuck happened and where did all the time go. If you're in your 20s right now, then 946,080,000 seconds sounds like a fuckload of time. Each of those 946 million seconds is a Now and I get that for some of them, you'll be asleep or on the toilet or whatever. I get that. There's still a lot of Nows left in there to really focus and make a difference. 946,080,000 is thirty years of Nows. Mine are almost up. 94 million to go and then I'm hopeful to get another 946 million more. I kinda promised my kids I'd live to one hundred years old.

Maybe getting what you want will be the third installment. Until then, kill your Trolls, stop blaming, stop living in fantasyland and get your shit done.

You fucking deserve it.

Thank you for reading this book. Independent self-publishing opens up a lot of opportunities for people to share their knowledge and expertise. This book was written and self-published by E.B. Davis II, a work of labor and love. Actually, writing the book wasn't the hard part. Dare I say it was actually fun. The hard part was birthing it into the world. Please consider taking a moment and leaving a review of this work on whichever platform from which it was purchased. Whatever you have to say about it, your thoughts and opinions matter. What you have to say could help someone else and make me a better writer. Either way, I support any person who is walking a personal path to a better self and a better life. These journeys are not easy and it helps to have a friendly face along the way. Sure, my words can be harsh but sometimes we don't hear until someone raises their voice. Raise your voice. Speak your truth. Do it with compassion.

39700769R00073

Made in the USA
Middletown, DE
19 March 2019